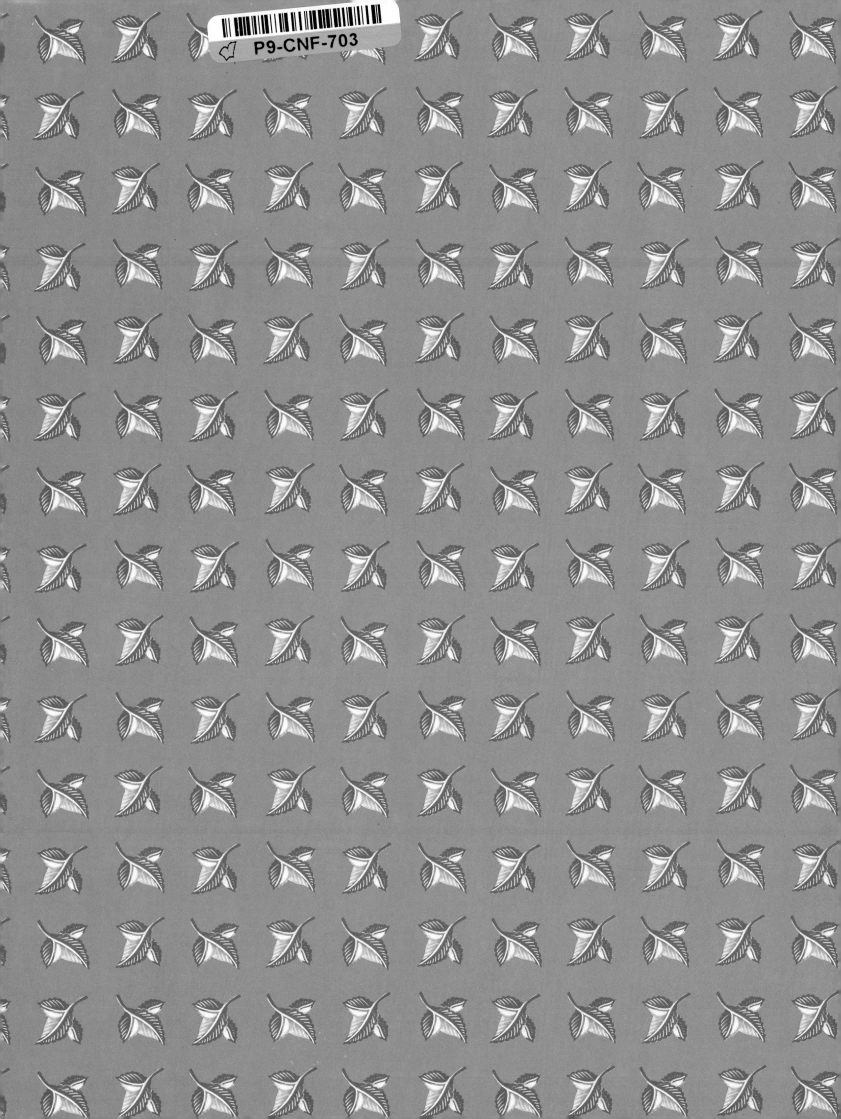

THE VEGETARIAN Gourmet

THE VEGETARIAN
Gourmet

HERMES
HOUSE

This edition published in 1998 by Hermes House
27 West 20th Street, New York, NY 10011

HERMES HOUSE books are available for bulk purchase for sales
promotion and for premium use. For details, write or call the sales
director, Hermes House, 27 West 20th Street, New York, NY 10011;
(800) 354-9657

Hermes House is an imprint of
Anness Publishing Limited

ISBN 1 84038 128 0

Publisher: Joanna Lorenz
Project Editor: Samantha Gray
Designer: Adrian Morris
Photographer: Michael Michaels
Home Economist: Wendy Lee

Previously published as part of a larger compendium,
The Ultimate Vegetarian Cookbook

Printed in Singapore by Star Standard Industries Pte. Ltd.

1 3 5 7 9 10 8 6 4 2

 THE LEAF SYMBOL NEXT TO A RECIPE INDICATES THAT IT IS SUITABLE FOR VEGANS.

CONTENTS

SOUPS
&
STARTERS

Tantalizing appetizers range from traditional favorites – including
soups that could be served either before a main course or on their own
as a light and wholesome meal – to more exotic dishes for elegant dinners.

Egg Flower Soup

For the very best flavor, you do need to use a home made stock for this soup. The egg sets into pretty strands giving the soup a flowery look, hence the name.

SERVES 6
4 cups stock
3 tbsp light soy sauce
2 tbsp dry sherry or vermouth
3 scallions, diagonally sliced
small piece fresh ginger root, shredded
4 large lettuce leaves, shredded
1 tsp sesame seed oil
2 eggs, beaten
salt and ground black pepper
sesame seeds, to garnish

1 Pour the stock into a large saucepan. Add all the ingredients except the eggs and seeds. Bring to a boil and then cook for about 2 minutes.

2 Very carefully, pour the eggs in a thin, steady stream into the center of the boiling liquid.

3 Count to three then quickly stir the soup. The egg will begin to cook and form long threads. Season to taste, ladle the soup into warm bowls and serve immediately sprinkled with sesame seeds.

Broccoli and Saga Blue Cheese Soup

A popular vegetable, broccoli makes a delicious soup with an appetizing deep green colour. For a tasty tang, stir in some cubes of Saga Blue cheese just before serving.

SERVES 6
1 onion, chopped
1 lb broccoli spears, chopped
1 large zucchini, chopped
1 large carrot, chopped
1 medium potato, chopped
2 tbsp butter
2 tbsp sunflower oil
8 cups stock or water
3 oz Saga Blue or Morbier cheese, cubed
salt and ground black pepper
almond flakes, to garnish (optional)

VARIATION

Try using cauliflower instead of broccoli in this recipe. Stilton also makes a tasty alternative to Saga Blue cheese.

1 Put all the vegetables into a large saucepan, together with the butter and oil plus about 3 tbsp stock or water.

2 Heat the ingredients until sizzling and stir well. Cover and cook gently for 15 minutes, shaking the pan occasionally, until all the vegetables soften.

3 Add the rest of the stock or water, season and bring to a boil, then cover and simmer gently for about 25–30 minutes.

4 Strain the vegetables and reserve the liquid. Purée the vegetables in a food processor or blender then return them to the pan with the reserved liquid.

5 Bring the soup back to a gentle boil and stir in the cheese until it melts. (Don't let the soup boil too hard or the cheese will become stringy.) Season to taste and garnish with a scattering of almond flakes.

Borscht

A simply stunning color, this classic Russian soup is ideal to serve when you want to make something a little different. The flavor matures and improves too if it is made the day before it is needed.

SERVES 6
1 onion, chopped
1 lb raw beets, peeled and chopped
1 large cooking apple, chopped
2 celery stalks, chopped
½ red pepper, chopped
4 oz mushrooms, chopped
2 tbsp butter
2 tbsp sunflower oil
8 cups stock or water
1 tsp cumin seeds
pinch dried thyme
1 large bay leaf
fresh lemon juice
salt and ground black pepper
⅔ cup sour cream
few sprigs fresh dill, to garnish

1 Place all the chopped vegetables into a large saucepan with the butter, oil and 3 tbsp of the stock or water. Cover and cook gently for about 15 minutes, shaking the pan occasionally.

2 Stir in the cumin seeds and cook for a minute, then add the remaining stock or water, dried thyme, bay leaf, lemon juice and seasoning.

3 Bring to a boil, then cover and turn down to a gentle simmer. Cook for about 30 minutes.

4 Strain the vegetables and reserve the liquid. Pass the vegetables through a food processor or blender until they are smooth and creamy.

5 Return the vegetables to the pan, stir in the reserved stock and reheat. Check the seasoning.

6 Serve the borscht with swirls of sour cream and topped with a few sprigs of fresh dill.

VARIATION

This soup can be served fairly thick, as long as the vegetables are finely chopped first.

Beets are something of an under-valued vegetable, although popular in many European countries. For example, they are delicious served as a hot vegetable accompaniment with a bechamel sauce and topped with crisp bread crumbs. Alternatively, try them raw and coarsely grated, then tossed in dressing for a side salad.

Garlicky Mushrooms

Serve these on toast for a quick and tasty starter, or pop them into small ramekins and serve with slices of warm crusty bread. Use some shiitake mushrooms, if you can find them, for a richer flavor.

SERVES 4
1 lb button mushrooms, sliced if large
3 tbsp olive oil
3 tbsp stock or water
2 tbsp dry sherry (optional)
3 garlic cloves, crushed
4 oz low fat farmer's cheese
2 tbsp fresh parsley, chopped
1 tbsp fresh chives, chopped
salt and ground black pepper

1 Put the mushrooms into a large saucepan with the olive oil, stock or water and sherry, if using. Heat until bubbling then cover and simmer for 5 minutes.

2 Add the garlic and stir well. Cook for a further 2 minutes. Remove the mushrooms with a slotted spoon and set them aside. Cook the liquor until it reduces down to 2 tbsp. Remove from the heat and stir in the cheese and herbs.

3 Stir the mixture well until the cheese melts, then return the mushrooms to the pan so that they become coated with the cheese mixture. Season to taste.

4 Pile the mushrooms onto thick slices of hot toast. Alternatively, spoon them into four ramekins and serve accompanied by slices of crusty bread.

Ricotta and Borlotti Bean Pâté

A lovely light yet full-flavored pâté. For an attractive presentation, spoon the pâté into small, oiled ring molds, turn out and fill with some whole borlotti beans, simply dressed with lemon juice, olive oil and fresh herbs.

SERVES 4
1 × 14 oz can borlotti beans, drained
1 garlic clove, crushed
6 oz ricotta cheese (or other cream cheese)
4 tbsp butter, melted
juice of ½ lemon
salt and ground black pepper
2 tbsp fresh parsley, chopped
1 tbsp fresh thyme or dill, chopped
TO SERVE
extra canned beans (optional)
fresh lemon juice, olive oil and chopped herbs (optional)
salad leaves, radish slices and few sprigs fresh dill, to garnish

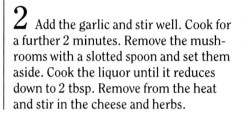

1 Blend the beans, garlic, cheese, butter, lemon juice and seasoning in a food processor until smooth.

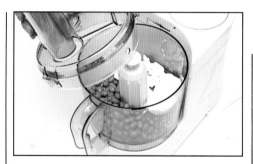

2 Add the chopped herbs and continue to blend. Spoon into one serving dish or four lightly oiled ramekins, the bases lined with discs of waxed paper. Chill the pâté so that it sets firm.

3 If serving with extra beans, dress them with lemon juice, olive oil and herbs, season well and spoon on top. Garnish with salad leaves and serve with warm crusty bread or toast.

4 If serving individually, turn each pâté out of its ramekin onto a small plate and remove the disc of paper. Garnish with salad leaves, and top the pâtés with radish slices and sprigs of dill.

VARIATION

You could try other canned beans for this recipe, although the softer lentils would not be suitable. Lima beans are surprisingly good. For an attractive presentation fill the center with dark red kidney beans and chopped fresh green beans.

Twice-baked Goat Cheese Soufflés

A good chef's trick is to reheat small baked soufflés out of their ramekins to serve with a salad. They puff up again and the outsides become nice and crispy. If you prefer, you can substitute another full-flavored cheese such as Cheddar or Parmesan.

SERVES 6
2 tbsp butter
3 tbsp all-purpose flour
1¼ cups hot milk
pinch cayenne pepper
squeeze of lemon juice
salt and ground black pepper
3½ oz semi-hard goat cheese, crumbled
2 eggs, separated
melted butter, for brushing
3 tbsp dried breadcrumbs
3 tbsp ground hazelnuts or walnuts
2 egg whites
salad garnish (optional)

1 Melt the butter and stir in the flour. Cook to a roux for a minute then gradually whisk in the hot milk to make a thick white sauce.

VARIATION

There is another good chef's trick – making soufflés in advance and chilling them unbaked. It helps to add an extra egg white or two when whisking, depending on the mixture. It is also possible to freeze unbaked soufflés in small ramekins and then to bake them from frozen, allowing an extra 5 or 10 minutes' baking time.

2 Simmer for a minute then season with cayenne, lemon juice, salt and pepper. Remove the pan from the heat and stir in the cheese until it melts. Cool slightly then beat in the egg yolks.

3 Brush the insides of six ramekins with the melted butter and coat them with the breadcrumbs and nuts mixed together. Shake out any excess.

4 Preheat the oven to 375°F and prepare a bain marie – a roasting pan half-filled with boiling water.

5 Whisk the four egg whites to the soft peak stage and carefully fold them into the main mixture using a figure of eight motion. Spoon into the ramekins.

6 Place the soufflés in the bain marie and bake for about 12–15 minutes until risen and golden brown. You can of course serve them at this stage; otherwise allow to cool then chill.

7 To serve twice-baked, reheat the oven to the same temperature. Run a knife round the inside of each ramekin and turn out each soufflé onto a baking tray.

8 Bake the soufflés for about 12 minutes. Serve on prepared plates with a dressed salad garnish.

Stuffed Artichokes 🌿

Artichokes are a little fussy to prepare but their delicious taste makes it all worthwhile, especially when they are stuffed with nuts, mushrooms and sun-dried tomatoes. This dish can be prepared in advance and reheated before serving.

SERVES 4
4 medium artichokes
salt
lemon slices
STUFFING
1 medium onion, chopped
1 garlic clove, crushed
3 tbsp olive oil
4 oz mushrooms, chopped
1 medium carrot, grated
1½ oz sun-dried tomatoes in oil, drained
    and sliced
leaves from a sprig of thyme
about 3–4 tbsp water
ground black pepper
2 cups fresh bread crumbs
extra olive oil, to cook
fresh parsley, chopped, to garnish

1 Boil the artichokes in plenty of salted water with a few slices of lemon for about 30 minutes, or until a leaf pulls easily from the base. Strain through a colander and cool the artichokes, setting them upside down.

2 To make the stuffing for the artichokes, gently fry the onion and garlic in the oil for 5 minutes, then add the mushrooms, carrot, sun-dried tomatoes and thyme.

3 Stir in the water, season well and cook for a further 5 minutes, then mix in the bread crumbs.

VARIATION

For a simpler meal, rather than stuff the artichokes, you could simply fill the centers with home made mayonnaise or serve with a dish of vinaigrette or melted butter for dipping the leaves.

4 Taking each artichoke in turn, pull the leaves apart and pull out the purple-tipped central leaves. Using a small teaspoon, scrape out the hairy choke, making sure that you remove it all.

5 Spoon the stuffing into the center of each artichoke, and push the leaves back into shape. Put the artichokes into an ovenproof dish and pour a little oil into the center of each one.

6 One-half hour before serving, heat the oven to 375°F and bake the artichokes for about 20–25 minutes until heated through. Serve garnished with a little chopped fresh parsley on top.

Bruschetta with Goat Cheese and Tapenade

Simple to prepare in advance, this appetizing dish can be served as a starter or at finger buffets. Make sure that you finely chop the ingredients for the tapenade.

SERVES 4–6
TAPENADE
1 × 14 oz can black olives, pitted and finely chopped
2 oz sun-dried tomatoes in oil, chopped
2 tbsp capers, chopped
1 tbsp green peppercorns, in brine, crushed
3–4 tbsp olive oil
2 garlic cloves, crushed
3 tbsp fresh basil, chopped, or 1 tsp dried basil
salt and ground black pepper
BASES
12 slices Ciabatta or other crusty bread
olive oil, for brushing
2 garlic cloves, halved
4 oz soft goat cheese (or plain cream cheese)
fresh herb sprigs, to garnish

1   Mix the tapenade ingredients all together and check the seasoning. It should not need too much. Allow to marinate overnight, if possible.

2   To make the bruschetta, grill both sides of the bread lightly until golden. Brush one side with oil and then rub with a cut clove of garlic. Set aside until ready to serve.

3   Spread the bruschetta with the cheese, roughing it up with a fork, and spoon the tapenade on top. Garnish with sprigs of herbs.

COOK'S TIP

The bruschetta is tastiest broiled over a open barbecue flame, if possible. Failing that a broiler will do, but avoid using a toaster – it gives too even a color and the bruschetta is supposed to have a smokey flavor.

Warm Avocadoes with Tangy Topping

Lightly grilled with a tasty topping of red onions and cheese, this dish makes a delightful alternative to the rather humdrum avocado vinaigrette.

SERVES 4
1 small red onion, sliced
1 garlic clove, crushed
1 tbsp sunflower oil
Worcestershire sauce
2 ripe avocados, halved and pitted
2 small tomatoes, sliced
1 tbsp fresh chopped basil, marjoram or parsley
2 oz Lancashire or Mozzarella cheese, sliced
salt and ground black pepper

1   Gently fry the onion and garlic in the oil for about 5 minutes until just softened. Shake in a little Worcestershire sauce.

2   Preheat a broiler. Place the avocado halves on the broiling pan and spoon the onions into the center.

3   Divide the tomato slices and fresh herbs between the four halves and top each one with the cheese.

4   Season well and broil until the cheese melts and starts to brown.

VARIATION

Avocadoes are wonderful served in other hot dishes too. Try them chopped and tossed into hot pasta or sliced and layered in a lasagne.

LIGHT LUNCHES & SUPPERS

For tempting lunches that are not too filling and tasty television suppers, experiment with these glorious recipes, from those that include protein-rich ingredients such as tofu to irresistible cheese and pasta dishes.

Mexican Brunch Eggs

Instead of eggs on toast, why not try them on fried corn tortillas with chilies and creamy avocado? Packaged tortillas are readily available from larger supermarkets or delicatessens.

SERVES 4
oil, for frying
8 tortilla corn pancakes
1 avocado
1 large tomato
4 tbsp butter
8 eggs
4 jalepeno chilies, either fresh or
   canned, sliced
salt and ground black pepper
1 tbsp fresh coriander, chopped,
   to garnish

1 Heat the oil and fry the tortillas for a few seconds each side. Remove and drain. Keep the tortillas warm.

2 Halve, pit and peel the avocado, then cut into slices. Dip the tomato into boiling water, then skin and chop roughly.

3 Melt the butter in a frying pan and fry the eggs, in batches, sunny side up.

4 Place two tortillas on four plates, slip an egg on each and top with sliced chilies, avocado and tomato. Season and serve garnished with fresh coriander.

Fried Tomatoes with Polenta Crust

If you saw the film "Fried Green Tomatoes" then you should enjoy this dish! No need to search for home-grown green tomatoes – any slightly under-ripe ones will do.

SERVES 4
4 large firm under-ripe tomatoes
1 cup polenta or coarse cornmeal
1 tsp dried oregano
½ tsp garlic powder
all-purpose flour, for dredging
1 egg, beaten with seasoning
oil, for deep fat frying

1 Cut the tomatoes into thick slices. Mix the polenta or cornmeal with the oregano and garlic powder.

2 Put the flour, egg and polenta or cornmeal into bowls. Dip the tomato slices into the flour, then into the egg and finally into the polenta or cornmeal.

3 Fill a shallow frying pan one-third full of oil and heat steadily until quite hot.

4 Slip the tomato slices into the oil carefully, a few at a time, and fry on each side until crisp. Remove and drain. Repeat with the remaining tomatoes, reheating the oil in between. Serve with salad.

Pissaladière

A French Mediterranean classic, this is a delicious and colorful tart full of punchy flavor. Ideally, put the base and fillings together just when serving so the base remains crisp.

SERVES 6
PASTRY
2 cups all-purpose flour
½ cup butter or sunflower margarine, chilled
1 tsp dried mixed herbs
pinch salt
FILLING
2 large onions, thinly sliced
2 garlic cloves, crushed
3 tbsp olive oil
fresh nutmeg, grated, to taste
1 × 14 oz can chopped tomatoes
1 tsp sugar
leaves from small sprig of thyme
salt and ground black pepper
⅔ cup pitted black olives, sliced
2 tbsp capers
fresh parsley, chopped, to garnish

1 Rub the flour with the butter or margarine until it forms fine crumbs, then mix in the herbs and salt. Mix to a firm dough with cold water. Preheat the oven to 375°F.

2 Roll out the crust and line a 9 in pie pan. Line with foil and dried beans and bake for 10 minutes. Remove foil and beans and bake for 5 minutes more.

3 Gently fry the onions and garlic in the oil for about 10 minutes until quite soft and mix in the nutmeg.

4 Stir in the tomatoes, sugar, thyme and seasoning and simmer gently for about 10 minutes until the mixture is reduced and slightly syrupy.

5 Remove from the heat and allow to cool. Mix in the olives and capers.

6 When ready to serve, spoon into the pie shell, sprinkle with some fresh chopped parsley and serve at room temperature.

VARIATION

To serve Pissaladière hot, top with grated cheese and broil until the cheese is golden and bubbling. The crisp-baked pastry shell can be used as a base for a number of other vegetable mixtures. Try filling it with a Russian Salad – chopped, cooked root vegetables, including potato and carrot, mixed with peas, beans and onions, blended with mayonnaise and sour cream. Top with slices of hard-boiled egg and garnish with chopped fresh herbs.

Multi Mushroom Stroganoff

A pan fry of sliced mushrooms swirled with sour cream is made especially interesting if two or three varieties of mushroom are used. It is even more delicious if you can incorporate woodland or wild mushrooms.

SERVES 3–4
3 tbsp olive oil
1 lb wild mushrooms (including ceps, shiitakes or oysters), sliced
3 scallions, sliced
2 garlic cloves, crushed
2 tbsp dry sherry or vermouth
salt and ground black pepper
1¼ cups sour cream or heavy cream
1 tbsp fresh marjoram or thyme leaves, chopped
fresh parsley, chopped

1 Heat the oil in a large frying pan and fry the mushrooms gently, stirring them occasionally until they are softened and just cooked.

2 Add the scallions, garlic and sherry or vermouth and cook for a minute more. Season well.

3 Stir in the sour cream or heavy cream and heat to just below boiling. Stir in the marjoram or thyme then scatter over the parsley. Serve with rice, pasta or boiled new potatoes.

Lima Bean and Pesto Pasta

Buy good quality, ready-made pesto, rather than making your own. Pesto forms the basis of several very tasty sauces, and it is especially good with lima beans.

SERVES 4
8 oz pasta shapes
salt and ground black pepper
fresh nutmeg, grated
2 tbsp extra virgin olive oil
1 × 14 oz can lima beans, drained
3 tbsp pesto sauce
⅔ cup light cream
TO SERVE
3 tbsp pine nuts
Parmesan cheese, grated (optional)
sprigs of fresh basil, to garnish (optional)

1 Boil the pasta until *al dente*, then drain, leaving it a little wet. Return the pasta to the pan, season, and stir in the nutmeg and oil.

2 Heat the beans in a saucepan with the pesto and cream, stirring until the cream begins to simmer. Toss the beans and pesto into the pasta and mix well.

3 Serve in bowls topped with pine nuts, and add a little grated cheese and basil sprigs if you wish.

Eggs Benedict with Quick Hollandaise

Traditional Hollandaise sauce is tricky to make without it curdling. To make it quickly, yet still achieve a thick and creamy sauce, use a blender or food processor. Hollandaise sauce is simply delicious served over poached eggs on hot toasted muffins.

SERVES 4
2 egg yolks
1 tsp dry mustard
good pinch each salt and ground black
   pepper
1 tbsp wine vinegar or lemon juice
¾ cup butter
4 muffins, split
butter or low fat spread
4 large eggs
2 tbsp capers
a little fresh parsley, chopped, to garnish

1 Blend the egg yolks with the mustard and seasoning in a blender or food processor for a few seconds until well mixed. Mix in the vinegar or lemon juice.

2 Heat the butter until it is on the point of bubbling then, with the machine still running, slowly pour the butter onto the egg yolks.

3 The mixture should emulsify instantly and become thick and creamy. Switch off the blender and set the sauce aside.

4 Toast the split muffins. Cut four of the halves in two and lightly butter. Place the four uncut halves on warmed plates and leave unbuttered.

5 Poach the eggs either in gently simmering water or in an egg poacher. Drain well and slip carefully onto the uncut muffin halves.

6 Spoon the sauce over the muffins and then sprinkle with capers and parsley. Serve immediately with the buttered muffin quarters.

VARIATION

This classic American brunch dish is said to have originated in New York, and is ideal to serve on a special occasion such as a birthday treat or New Year's day.

Instead of the toasted muffin, you could make more of a main meal by serving the dish on a bed of lightly steamed or blanched spinach mixed with quick fried sliced mushrooms and onions. The quick Hollandaise sauce is of course ideal as an all-purpose serving sauce for vegetables, baked potatoes, cauliflower and broccoli.

Quick Basmati and Nut Pilaf 🌿

Light and fragrant basmati rice from the foothills of the Himalayas cooks perfectly using this simple pilaf method. Use whatever nuts are your favorite – even unsalted peanuts are good, although almonds, cashews or pistachios are more exotic.

SERVES 4–6
1¼ cups basmati rice
1 onion, chopped
1 garlic clove, crushed
1 large carrot, coarsely grated
1–2 tbsp sunflower oil
1 tsp cumin seeds
2 tsp ground coriander
2 tsp black mustard seeds (optional)
4 cardamom pods
2 cups stock or water
1 bay leaf
salt and ground black pepper
½ cup unsalted nuts
fresh parsley or coriander, chopped, to garnish

RINSING BASMATI

For light, fluffy grains basmati rice is best rinsed before cooking to remove any surface starch. The traditional method is to put the rice into a large bowl of cold water. Swill the grains around with your hands, then tip out the cloudy water. (The rice will quickly sink to the bottom). Repeat this action about five times. Ideally, leave the rice to soak for 30 minutes in the last rinsing water. This ensures a lighter, fluffier grain.

1 Wash the rice either by the traditional Indian method (see below) or in a sieve under a running tap. If there is time, soak the rice for 30 minutes, then drain well in a sieve.

2 In a large shallow pan, gently fry the onion, garlic and carrot in the oil for a few minutes.

3 Stir in the rice and spices and cook for a further minute or two so that that the grains are coated in oil.

4 Pour in the stock or water, add the bay leaf and season well. Bring to a boil, cover and simmer very gently for about 10 minutes.

5 Remove from the heat without lifting the lid – this helps the rice to firm up and cook further. Leave for about 5 minutes.

6 If the rice is cooked, there will be small steam holes in the center. Discard the bay leaf and cardamom pods.

7 Stir in the nuts and check the seasoning. Scatter the mixture with the chopped parsley or coriander. This whole dish can be made ahead and reheated.

Spaghetti with Feta

We think of pasta as being essentially Italian but, in fact, the Greeks have a great appetite for it too and it complements beautifully the tangy, full-flavoured feta cheese.

SERVES 2
4 oz spaghetti
1 garlic clove
2 tbsp extra virgin olive oil
8 cherry tomatoes, halved
a little freshly grated nutmeg
salt and ground black pepper
3 oz feta cheese, crumbled
1 tbsp chopped fresh basil
a few black olives (optional), to serve

1 Boil the spaghetti in plenty of lightly salted water according to the instructions on the package, then drain.

2 In the same pan gently heat the garlic clove in the oil for a minute or two then add the cherry tomatoes.

3 Increase the heat to fry the tomatoes lightly for a minute, then remove the garlic and discard.

4 Toss in the spaghetti, add nutmeg and seasoning to taste and then stir in the crumbled feta and basil.

5 Check the seasoning, remembering that feta can be quite salty, and serve hot topped with olives if liked.

Potatoes with Blue Cheese and Walnuts

We are so used to eating potatoes as a side dish, we forget they can be a good main meal too. This dish is so versatile it can be served as either. Use Stilton, Danish Blue, Roquefort or any other blue veined cheese.

SERVES 4
1 lb small new potatoes
small head of celery, sliced
small red onion, sliced
4 oz blue cheese, mashed
⅔ cup light cream
salt and ground black pepper
½ cup walnut pieces
2 tbsp fresh parsley, chopped

1 Cover the potatoes with water and boil for about 15 minutes, adding the sliced celery and onion to the pan for the last 5 minutes or so.

2 Drain the vegetables and put them into a shallow serving dish.

3 In a small saucepan melt the cheese in the cream, slowly, stirring occasionally. Do not allow the mixture to boil but heat it until it scalds.

4 Season the sauce to taste. Pour it over the vegetables and scatter over the walnuts and parsley. Serve hot.

MAIN COURSES

Create healthy and satisfying meals that make the most of the wonderful variety of herbs and spices, as well as nutritious ingredients such as lentils, rice and vegetables.

Sprouting Beans and Pak Choi

Supermarkets are fast becoming cosmopolitan and many stock exotic varieties of vegetables.

SERVES 4
3 tbsp groundnut oil
3 scallions, sliced
2 garlic cloves, cut in slivers
1 in cube fresh ginger root
ginger, cut in slivers
1 carrot, cut in thin sticks
5 oz sprouting beans (e.g. lentils, mung beans, chick peas)
1 × 7 oz pak choi cabbage, shredded
½ cup unsalted cashew nuts or halved almonds
SAUCE
3 tbsp light soy sauce
2 tbsp dry sherry
1 tbsp sesame oil
⅔ cup cold water
1 tsp corn starch
1 tsp honey
ground black pepper

1 Heat the oil in a large wok and stir-fry the onions, garlic, ginger and carrot for 2 minutes. Add the sprouting beans and fry for another 2 minutes, stirring and tossing them together.

2 Add the pak choi and nuts or almonds and stir-fry until the cabbage leaves are just wilting. Quickly mix all the sauce ingredients together in a jug and pour them into the wok, stirring immediately.

3 The vegetables will be coated in a thin, glossy sauce. Season and serve as soon as possible.

Thai Tofu Curry

Thai food is a marvelous mixture of Chinese and Indian styles, plus other delicious ingredients.

SERVES 4
2 × 7 oz packages tofu curd, cubed
2 tbsp light soy sauce
2 tbsp groundnut oil
PASTE
1 small onion, chopped
2 fresh green chilies, seeded and chopped
2 garlic cloves, chopped
1 tbsp grated fresh galingale or 1 tsp grated fresh ginger
2 kaffir lime leaves or 1 tsp lime rind, grated
2 tsp coriander berries, crushed
2 tsp cumin seeds, crushed
3 tbsp fresh coriander, chopped
1 tbsp Thai fish sauce (Nam pla) or soy sauce
juice of 1 lime or small lemon
1 tsp sugar
1 oz creamed coconut dissolved in ⅔ cup boiling water
GARNISH
thin slices fresh red chili or red pepper
fresh coriander leaves

1 Toss the tofu cubes in soy sauce and leave to marinate for 15 minutes or so while you prepare the paste.

2 Put all the paste ingredients into a food processor and grind until smooth.

3 To cook, heat the oil in a wok until quite hot. Drain the tofu cubes and stir-fry them at a high temperature until they are well browned on all sides and just firm. Drain on paper towel.

4 Wipe out the wok. Pour in the paste and stir well. Return the tofu to the wok and mix it into the paste, reheating the ingredients as you stir.

5 Serve this dish on a flat platter garnished with red chili or pepper and chopped coriander. Bowls of Thai fragrant or jasmine rice are the perfect accompaniment to the curry.

Festive Jalousie

An excellent puff pastry pie to serve either on Christmas Day or at anytime during the holiday period. Chinese dried chestnuts make an excellent substitute for fresh ones when soaked and cooked. Or you could drain a can of chestnuts.

SERVES 6
1 lb puff pastry, thawed if frozen
1 lb Brussels sprouts, trimmed
about 16 whole chestnuts, peeled if fresh
1 large red pepper, sliced
1 large onion, sliced
3 tbsp sunflower oil
1 large egg yolk, beaten with 1 tbsp
   water
SAUCE
scant ½ cup all-purpose flour
3 tbsp butter
½ pint milk
3 oz Cheddar cheese, grated
2 tbsp dry sherry
good pinch dried sage
salt and ground black pepper
3 tbsp fresh parsley, chopped

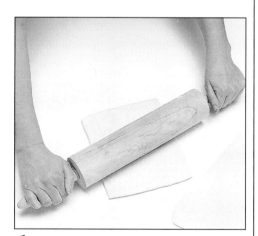

1 Roll out the pastry to make two large rectangles, roughly the size of your dish. The pastry should be about ¼ in thick and one rectangle should be slightly larger than the other. Set the pastry aside in the refrigerator.

2 Blanch the Brussels sprouts for 4 minutes in 1¼ cups boiling water, then drain them thoroughly, reserving the water. Refresh the sprouts under cold running water.

3 Cut each chestnut in half. Lightly fry the red pepper and onion in the oil for 5 minutes. Set aside till later.

4 Make up the sauce by beating the flour, butter and milk together over a medium heat. Beat the sauce continuously, bringing it to the boil, stirring until it is thickened and smooth.

5 Stir in the reserved sprout water, and the cheese, sherry, sage and seasoning. Simmer for 3 minutes to reduce and mix in the parsley.

6 Fit the larger piece of pastry into the pie dish and layer the sprouts, chestnuts, peppers and onions on top. Trickle over the sauce, making sure it seeps through to wet the vegetables.

7 Brush the pastry edges with beaten egg yolk and fit the second pastry sheet on top, pressing the edges well to seal them.

8 Crimp, press up the edges then mark the center. Glaze well all over with egg yolk. Set aside to rest somewhere cool while you preheat the oven to 400°F. Bake for 30–40 minutes until golden brown and crisp.

Greek Spinach Pies

These little horns of filo pastry are stuffed with a simple spinach and feta cheese filling to make a quick and easy main course.

SERVES 8
8 oz fresh leaf spinach, well washed
2 scallions, chopped
6 oz feta cheese, crumbled
1 egg, beaten
1 tbsp fresh dill, chopped
ground black pepper
4 large sheets or 8 small sheets of filo pastry
olive oil, for brushing

COOK'S TIP

The pies can be prepared ahead and chilled for a day or two, before baking and serving warm. Alternatively, open freeze on a wire rack, then wrap well in foil or plastic wrap and freeze for up to one month. Uncover and thaw well before baking as the recipe above.

1 Preheat the oven to 375°F. Blanch the spinach in the tiniest amount of water until just wilted, then drain very well, pressing it through a sieve with the back of a wooden spoon.

2 Chop the spinach finely and mix with the onions, feta, egg, dill and ground black pepper.

3 Lay out a sheet of filo pastry and brush with olive oil. If large, cut the pieces in two and sandwich them together. If small, fit another sheet on top and brush with olive oil.

4 Spread a quarter of the filling on one edge of the filo at the bottom, then roll it up firmly, but not too tightly. Shape into a crescent and place on a baking sheet.

5 Brush the pastry well with oil and bake for about 20–25 minutes in the preheated oven until golden and crisp. Cool slightly then remove to a wire rack to cool further.

Chunky Vegetable Paella

This Spanish rice dish has become a firm family favorite the world over. There are very many versions: here is one with eggplant and chick peas.

SERVES 6
good pinch saffron strands
1 eggplant, cut in thick chunks
salt
6 tbsp olive oil
1 large onion, sliced
3 garlic cloves, crushed
1 yellow pepper, sliced
1 red pepper, sliced
2 tsp paprika
1¼ cups Arborio rice
2½ cups stock
1 lb fresh tomatoes, skinned and chopped
ground black pepper
4 oz sliced mushrooms
4 oz cut green beans
1 × 15 oz can chick peas

1 Steep the saffron in 3 tbsp hot water. Sprinkle the eggplant with salt, leave to drain in a colander for 30 minutes, then rinse and dry.

2 In a large paella or frying pan, heat the oil and fry the onion, garlic, peppers and eggplant for about 5 minutes, stirring occasionally. Sprinkle in the paprika and stir again.

3 Mix in the rice, then pour in the stock, tomatoes, saffron and seasoning. Bring to a boil then simmer for 15 minutes, uncovered, shaking the pan frequently and stirring occasionally.

4 Stir in the mushrooms, green beans and chick peas (with the liquor). Continue cooking for a further 10 minutes, then serve hot from the pan.

Green Lentil Kulbyaka

This traditional Russian dish, usually made with fish and dough, can be adapted to make a light, crisp vegetarian centerpiece using filo pastry and green lentils.

SERVES 6
1 cup green lentils, soaked for 30 minutes
2 bay leaves
2 onions, sliced
5 cups stock
¾ cup butter, melted
1¼ cups long grain rice, ideally basmati
salt and ground black pepper
4 tbsp fresh parsley, chopped
2 tbsp fresh dill, chopped
1 egg, beaten
8 oz mushrooms, sliced
about 8 sheets filo pastry
3 eggs, hard-boiled and sliced

1 Drain the lentils then simmer with the bay leaves, one onion and half the stock for 25 minutes until cooked and thick. Season well, cool and set aside.

VARIATION

You could use a vegetarian puff pastry. In this case, use two blocks of pastry, placing one on top of the other and rolling to a large rectangle. Alternatively, you could make two separate kulbyakas. Divide the filling between the pastry and seal the edges well, glazing the tops with beaten egg.

2 Gently fry the remaining onion in another saucepan with 2 tbsp of the butter for 5 minutes. Stir in the rice, then the rest of the stock.

3 Season, bring to the boil, then cover and cook gently for 12 minutes for basmati, 15 minutes for long grain. Leave to stand, uncovered, for 5 minutes, then stir in the fresh herbs. Cool, then beat in the raw egg.

4 Fry the mushrooms in 3 tbsp of the butter for 5 minutes until they are just soft. Cool and set aside.

5 Brush the inside of a large, shallow ovenproof dish with more butter. Lay the sheets of filo in it, covering the base and making sure most of the pastry overhangs the sides. Brush well with butter in between and overlapping the pastry as required. Ensure there is a lot of pastry to fold over the mounded filling.

6 Into the pastry lining, layer rice, lentils and mushrooms, repeating the layers at least once and tucking the sliced egg in between. Season as you layer and form an even mound of filling.

7 Bring up the sheets of pastry over the filling, scrunching the top into attractive folds. Brush all over with the rest of the butter and set aside to chill and firm up.

8 Preheat the oven to 375°F. When ready, bake the kulbyaka for about 45 minutes until golden and crisp. Allow to stand for 10 minutes before you cut it and serve.

Chili con Queso

Known as a "bowl of red," this classic Mexican dish is just as tasty when made with all-red beans. For an extra good flavor, use small cubes of smoked cheese, and serve with rice. Epazote is a traditional Mexican herb found in specialist stores.

SERVES 4
2 cups red kidney beans, soaked and drained
3 tbsp sunflower oil
1 onion, chopped
1 red pepper, chopped
2 garlic cloves, crushed
1 fresh red chili, chopped (optional)
1 tbsp chili powder (mild or hot)
1 tsp ground cumin
4 cups stock or water
1 tsp crushed dried epazote leaves (optional)
ground black pepper
salt
1 tsp granulated sugar
4 oz cheese, cubed, to serve

1 Rinse the beans. In a large saucepan heat the oil and gently fry the onion, pepper, garlic and fresh chili for about 5 minutes.

2 Stir in the spices and cook for another minute, then add the beans, stock or water, epazote (if using) and a grinding of pepper. Don't add salt at this stage.

3 Boil for 10 minutes, cover and turn down to a gentle simmer. Cook for about 50 minutes checking the water level and adding extra if necessary.

4 When the beans are tender, season them well with salt. Remove about a quarter of the mixture and mash to a pulp or pass through a food processor.

5 Return the purée to the pan and stir well. Add sugar and serve hot with the cheese sprinkled on top. Great with plain boiled long-grain rice.

Big Barley Bowl

Barley seems to have slipped from fashion in recent years – a pity as it is a delicious grain with a marvelous nutty texture. Serve this with crisp cheese croûtes.

SERVES 6
1 red onion, sliced
½ fennel bulb, sliced
2 carrots, cut in sticks
1 parsnip, sliced
3 tbsp sunflower oil
1 cup pearl barley
4 cups stock
1 tsp dried thyme
fresh parsley, chopped, to garnish
salt and ground black pepper
⅔ cup green beans, sliced
1 × 15 oz can pinto beans, drained
CROÛTES
1 medium sized baguette, sliced
olive oil, for brushing
1 garlic clove, cut in half
4 tbsp grated Parmesan cheese

1 In a large, heatproof casserole, sauté the onion, fennel, carrots and parsnip gently in the oil for 10 minutes.

2 Stir in the barley and stock. Bring to a boil, add the herbs and seasoning, then cover and simmer gently for 40 minutes.

3 Stir in the green beans and pinto beans and continue cooking – covered – for a further 20 minutes.

4 Meanwhile, preheat the oven to 375°F. Brush the baguette slices lightly with olive oil and then place them on a baking sheet.

5 Bake for about 15 minutes until light golden and crisp. Remove from the oven and quickly rub each croûte with the garlic halves. Sprinkle over the cheese and return to the oven to melt.

6 Ladle the barley into warm bowls and serve sprinkled with parsley, accompanied by the cheese croûtes. This dish is best eaten with a spoon.

Vegetables Julienne with Red Pepper Coulis

Just the right course for those watching their weight. Choose a selection of as many vegetables as you feel you can eat. Cut them into equal size finger lengths and steam them over aromatic, bubbling water.

SERVES 2

A selection of vegetables. Choose from:
  carrots, turnips, asparagus, parsnips, zucchini, green beans, broccoli, salsify, cauliflower, snow peas

RED PEPPER COULIS

1 small onion, chopped
1 garlic clove, crushed
1 tbsp sunflower oil
1 tbsp water
3 red peppers, roasted, skinned and chopped
8 tbsp low fat ricotta
squeeze of fresh lemon juice
salt and ground black pepper
sprigs of fresh thyme
2 bay leaves
fresh green herbs, to garnish

2 Make the coulis: lightly sauté the onion and garlic in the oil and water for 3 minutes then add the peppers and cook for a further 2 minutes.

3 Pass the coulis through a food processor, then work in the ricotta, lemon juice and seasoning.

4 Boil some salted water with the fresh thyme and bay leaves, and fit a steamer over the top.

5 Arrange the prepared vegetables on the steamer, placing the harder root vegetables at the bottom and steaming these for about 3 minutes.

6 Add the other vegetables according to their natural tenderness and cook for a further 2–4 minutes.

7 Serve the vegetables on plates with the sauce to one side. Garnish with fresh green herbs, if you wish.

1 Prepare the vegetables by cutting them into thin fingers or small, even bite size pieces.

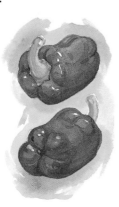

VARIATION

The red pepper coulis makes a wonderful sauce for many other dishes. Try it spooned over fresh pasta with lightly steamed or fried zucchini, or use it as a pouring sauce for savory filled crêpes.

Curried Parsnip Pie

Sweet, creamy parsnips are beautifully complemented by the addition of curry spices and cheese. This unusual but delicious combination of flavors makes for a very tasty pie.

SERVES 4

PASTRY
½ cup butter or margarine
1 cup all-purpose flour
salt and ground black pepper
1 tsp dried thyme or oregano
cold water, to mix

FILLING
8 baby onions, or shallots, peeled
2 large parsnips, thinly sliced
2 carrots, thinly sliced
2 tbsp butter or margarine
2 tbsp whole wheat flour
1 tbsp mild curry or tikka paste
1¼ cups milk
4 oz sharp cheese, grated
salt and ground black pepper
3 tbsp fresh coriander or parsley, chopped
1 egg yolk, beaten with 2 tsp water

1 Make the pastry by rubbing the butter or margarine into the flour until it resembles fine breadcrumbs. Season and stir in the thyme or oregano, then mix to a firm dough with cold water.

2 Blanch the baby onions or shallots with the parsnips and carrots in just enough water to cover, for about 5 minutes. Drain, reserving about 1¼ cups of the liquid.

3 In a clean pan, melt the butter or margarine, and stir in the flour and spice paste to make a roux. Gradually whisk in the reserved stock and milk until smooth. Simmer for a minute or two.

4 Take the pan off the heat, stir in the cheese and seasoning, then mix into the vegetables with the coriander or parsley.

COOK'S TIP

This pie freezes well and makes a good stand-by for a mid-week meal. For best results, make up to the final stage and freeze unbaked. Open freeze until solid, then wrap well in freezer plastic wrap, seal and label. Use within one month.

Cauliflower, broccoli or any other favorite vegetable can be added to the filling to give a variety of flavors and textures.

5 Pour into a pie dish, fix a pie funnel in the center and allow to cool.

6 Roll out the pastry, large enough to fit the top of the pie dish. Re-roll the trimmings into long strips.

7 Brush the pastry edges with egg yolk wash and fit on the pastry strips. Brush again with egg yolk wash.

8 Using a rolling pin, lift the rolled out pastry over the pie top and fit over the funnel, pressing it down well onto the strips underneath.

9 Cut off the overhanging pastry and crimp the edges. Cut a hole for the funnel, brush all over well with the remaining egg yolk wash and make decorations with the trimmings, glazing them too.

10 Place the pie dish on a baking sheet and chill for 30 minutes while you preheat the oven to 400°F. Bake the pie for about 25–30 minutes until golden brown and crisp on top.

Vegetables under a Light Creamy Crust

This light main course dish is ideal for a summer supper. The subtle flavours of leeks, zucchini and mushrooms are topped by a tasty crust of ricotta, Parmesan cheese and bread crumbs.

SERVES 4
2 leeks, thinly sliced
3 zucchini, thickly sliced
12 oz sliced mushrooms, including oyster
   and shiitake mushrooms
2 garlic cloves, crushed
2 tbsp olive oil
2 tbsp butter
1 tbsp all-purpose flour
1¼ cups stock
1 tsp dried thyme
salt and ground black pepper
2 tbsp ricotta cheese
TOPPING
1 lb ricotta cheese
2 tbsp butter, melted
3 eggs, beaten
salt and ground black pepper
fresh nutmeg, grated
freshly grated Parmesan cheese and
   dried bread crumbs, to sprinkle

1 Preheat the oven to 375°F. In a saucepan, gently fry the leeks, zucchini, mushrooms and garlic in the oil and butter for about 7 minutes, stirring occasionally, until the vegetables are just soft.

2 Stir in the flour, then gradually mix in the stock. Bring to a boil, stirring until thickened. Add the thyme and seasoning. Take the pan off the heat and stir in the ricotta. Pour the vegetable mixture into a shallow ovenproof dish.

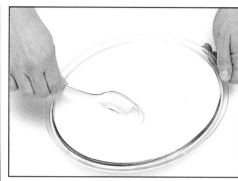

3 Beat the topping ingredients together, seasoning them well and adding the nutmeg to taste. Spoon on top of the vegetables and sprinkle with Parmesan cheese and bread crumbs.

4 Bake for about 30 minutes until a light golden, firm crust forms. Serve hot with pasta or crusty bread.

Potato and Parsnip Amandine

Shells of baked potatoes are filled with a spicy parsnip and crunchy almond mix. They make an unusual alternative to plain baked potatoes.

SERVES 4
4 large baking potatoes
olive oil, for greasing
8 oz parsnips, diced
2 tbsp butter
1 tsp cumin seeds
1 tsp ground coriander
2 tbsp light cream or natural yogurt
salt and ground black pepper
4 oz Gruyère or Cheddar cheese, grated
1 egg, beaten
¼ cup flaked almonds

1 Rub the potatoes all over with oil, score in half, then bake at 400°F for about 1 hour until cooked.

2 Meanwhile, boil the parsnips until tender, then drain well, mash and mix with the butter, spices and cream or natural yogurt.

3 When the potatoes are cooked, halve, scoop out and mash the flesh then mix with the parsnip, seasoning well.

4 Stir in the cheese, egg and three quarters of the almonds. Fill the potato shells with the mixture and sprinkle over the remaining almonds.

5 Return to the oven and bake for about 15–20 minutes until golden brown and the filling has set lightly. Serve hot with a side salad.

Baked Pumpkin

Glorious pumpkin shells evoke the delights of the fall season and seem too good simply to throw away. Use one instead as a serving pot. Pumpkin and pasta make marvellous partners, especially as a main course served from the baked shell.

SERVES 4
1 × 4 lb pumpkin
1 onion, sliced
1 in cube fresh ginger root
3 tbsp extra virgin olive oil
1 zucchini, sliced
4 oz sliced mushrooms
1 × 14 oz can chopped tomatoes
1 cup pasta shells
2 cups stock
salt and ground black pepper
4 tbsp ricotta cheese
2 tbsp fresh basil, chopped

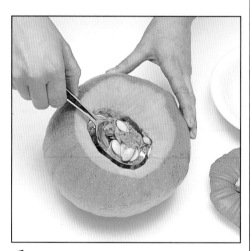

1 Preheat the oven to 350°F. Cut the top off the pumpkin with a large, sharp knife, then scoop out and discard all the seeds.

2 Using a small, sharp knife and a sturdy tablespoon extract as much of the pumpkin flesh as possible, then chop it into chunks.

3 Bake the pumpkin with its lid on for 45 minutes to one hour until the inside begins to soften.

4 Meanwhile, make the filling. Gently fry the onion, ginger and pumpkin flesh in the olive oil for about 10 minutes, stirring occasionally.

5 Add the zucchini and mushrooms and cook for a further 3 minutes, then stir in the tomatoes, pasta shells and stock. Season well, bring to a boil, then cover and simmer gently for 10 minutes.

6 Stir the ricotta cheese and basil into the pasta and spoon the mixture into the pumpkin. It may not be possible to fit all the filling into the pumpkin shell, so serve the rest separately if this is the case.

Festive Lentil and Nut Roast

An excellent celebration dish which can be served with all the trimmings, including vegetarian gravy. Garnish it with fresh cranberries and French parsley for a really festive effect.

SERVES 6–8
⅔ cup red lentils
1 cup hazelnuts
1 cup walnuts
1 large carrot
2 celery stalks
1 large onion
4 oz mushrooms
4 tbsp butter
2 tsp mild curry powder
2 tbsp tomato ketchup
2 tbsp Worcestershire sauce
1 egg, beaten
2 tsp salt
4 tbsp fresh parsley, chopped
⅔ cup water

1 Soak the lentils for 1 hour in cold water then drain well. Grind the nuts in a food processor until quite fine but not too smooth. Set the nuts aside.

2 Chop the carrot, celery, onion and mushrooms into small chunks, then pass them through a food processor or blender until they are quite finely chopped.

3 Fry the vegetables gently in the butter for 5 minutes, then stir in the curry powder and cook for a minute. Cool.

4 Meanwhile, mix the soaked lentils with the nuts, vegetables, ketchup, Worcestershire sauce, egg, salt, parsley and water.

5 Grease and line the base and sides of a long 2 lb loaf pan with waxed paper or a sheet of foil. Press the mixture firmly into the pan and smooth the surface. Preheat the oven to 375°F.

6 Bake for about 1–1¼ hours until just firm, covering the top with a butter paper or piece of foil if it starts to burn.

7 Allow the mixture to stand for about 15 minutes before you turn it out and peel off the paper. It will be fairly soft when cut as it is a moist loaf.

Vegetarian Gravy

Make up a large batch of this and freeze it in small containers ready to reheat and serve. A delicious alternative to the meat version.

MAKES ABOUT 1¾ PINTS
1 large red onion, sliced
3 turnips, sliced
3 celery stalks, sliced
4 oz mushrooms, halved
2 whole garlic cloves
6 tbsp sunflower oil
6 cups vegetable stock or water
3 tbsp soy sauce
good pinch of granulated sugar
salt and ground black pepper

1 Cook the vegetables and garlic on a moderately high heat with the oil in a large saucepan, stirring occasionally until nicely browned but not singed. This should take about 15–20 minutes.

2 Add the stock or water and soy sauce and bring to a boil, then cover and simmer for another 20 minutes.

3 Purée the vegetables, adding a little of the stock, and return them to the pan by rubbing the pulp through a sieve with the back of a ladle or wooden spoon.

4 Taste for seasoning and add the sugar. Freeze at least half of the gravy to use later and reheat the rest to serve with the lentil and nut roast.

Homemade Ravioli

It is a pleasure to make your own fresh pasta and you might be surprised at just how easy it is to fill and shape ravioli. Allow a little extra time than you would for ready-made or dried pasta. A food processor will save you time and effort in making and kneading the dough. A pasta rolling machine helps with the rolling out, but both these jobs can be done by hand if necessary.

SERVES 6
1½ cups all-purpose flour
½ tsp salt
1 tbsp olive oil
2 eggs, beaten
FILLING
1 small red onion, finely chopped
1 small green pepper, finely chopped
1 carrot, coarsely grated
1 tbsp olive oil
½ cup walnuts, chopped
4 oz ricotta cheese
2 tbsp fresh Parmesan or Pecorino cheese, grated
1 tbsp fresh marjoram or basil, chopped
salt and ground black pepper
extra oil or melted butter, to serve

1 Sift the flour and salt into a food processor. With the machine running, trickle in the oil and eggs and blend to a stiff but smooth dough.

2 Allow the machine to run for at least a minute if possible, otherwise remove the dough and knead it by hand for 5 minutes.

3 If using a pasta machine, break off small balls of dough and then feed them through the rollers a number of times, according to the manufacturer's instructions.

4 If rolling the pasta by hand, divide the dough into two. With a rolling pin roll out on a lightly floured surface to a thickness of about ¼ in.

5 Fold the pasta into three and re-roll. Repeat this up to six times until the dough is smooth and no longer sticky. Roll the pasta a little more thinly each time.

6 Keep the rolled dough under clean, dry dish towels while you complete the rest and make the filling. You should aim to have an even number of pasta sheets, all the same size if rolling by machine.

7 Fry the onion, pepper and carrot in the oil for 5 minutes, then allow to cool. Mix with the walnuts, cheeses, herbs and seasoning.

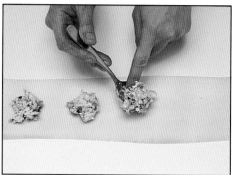

8 Lay out a pasta sheet and place small scoops of the filling in neat rows about 2 in apart. Brush in between with a little water and then place another pasta sheet on the top.

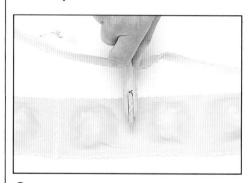

9 Press down well in between the rows then, using a ravioli or pastry cutter, cut into squares. If the edges pop open occasionally, press them back gently with your fingers.

10 Leave the ravioli to dry in the refrigerator, then boil in plenty of lightly salted water for just 5 minutes.

11 Toss the cooked ravioli in a little oil or melted butter before serving with either home made tomato sauce or some extra cheese.

Artichoke and Leek Crêpes

Fill wafer-thin crêpes with a mouth-watering soufflé mixture of Jerusalem artichokes and leek to serve for a special main course.

SERVES 4
1 cup all-purpose flour
pinch of salt
1 egg
1¼ cups milk
oil, for brushing
SOUFFLÉ FILLING
1 lb Jerusalem artichokes, peeled and diced
1 large leek, sliced thinly
4 tbsp butter
2 tbsp self-rising flour
2 tbsp light cream
3 oz sharp Cheddar cheese, grated
2 tbsp fresh parsley, chopped
fresh nutmeg, grated
2 eggs, separated
salt and ground black pepper

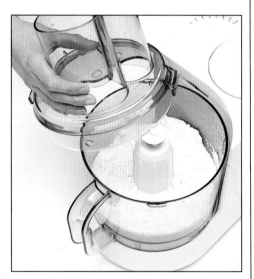

1 Make the crêpe batter by blending the flour, salt, egg and milk to a smooth batter in a food processor or blender.

2 Using a crêpe or omelette pan with a diameter of about 8 in, make a batch of thin pancakes. You will need about 2 tbsp of batter for each one.

3 Stack the pancakes under a clean dish towel as you make them. Reserve eight for this dish and freeze the rest.

4 Cook the artichokes and leek with the butter in a covered saucepan on a gentle heat for about 12 minutes until very soft. Mash with the back of a wooden spoon. Season well.

5 Stir the flour into the vegetables and cook for 1 minute. Take the pan off the heat and beat in the cream, cheese, parsley and nutmeg to taste. Cool, then add the egg yolks.

6 Whisk the egg whites until they form soft peaks and carefully fold them into the leek/artichoke mixture.

7 Lightly grease a small ovenproof dish and preheat the oven to 375°F. Fold each pancake in four, hold the top open and then carefully spoon the filling mixture into the center.

8 Arrange the crêpes in the prepared dish with the filling uppermost if possible. Bake for about 15 minutes until risen and golden. Eat immediately!

COOK'S TIP

Make sure the pan is at a good steady heat and is well oiled before you pour in the batter. It should sizzle as it hits the pan. Swirl the batter round to coat the pan, and then cook quickly.

Mushroom Gougère

A savory choux pastry ring makes a marvelous main course dish that can be made ahead then baked when required. Why not try it for a dinner party? It looks so very special.

SERVES 4
½ cup all-purpose flour
½ tsp salt
6 tbsp butter
¾ cup cold water
3 eggs, beaten
¾ cup diced Gruyère or aged Gouda cheese
FILLING
1 small onion, sliced
1 carrot, coarsely grated
8 oz button mushrooms, sliced
3 tbsp butter or margarine
1 tsp tikka or mild curry paste
2 tbsp all-purpose flour
1¼ cups milk
2 tbsp fresh parsley, chopped
salt and ground black pepper
2 tbsp flaked almonds

---

1 Preheat the oven to 400°F. Grease a shallow ovenproof dish approximately 9 in long.

2 To make the choux pastry, first sift the flour and salt onto a large sheet of waxed paper.

3 In a large saucepan, heat the butter and water until the butter just melts. Do not let the water boil. Fold the paper and shoot the flour into the pan all at once.

4 With a wooden spoon, beat the mixture rapidly until the lumps become smooth and the mixture comes away from the sides of the pan. Cool for 10 minutes.

5 Beat the eggs gradually into the mixture until you have a soft, but still quite stiff, dropping consistency. You may not need all the egg.

6 Stir in the cheese, then spoon the mixture round the sides of the greased ovenproof dish.

7 To make the filling, sauté the onion, carrot and mushrooms in the butter or margarine for 5 minutes. Stir in the curry paste then the flour.

8 Gradually stir in the milk and heat until thickened. Mix in the parsley, season well, then pour into the center of the choux pastry.

9 Bake for 35–40 minutes until risen and golden brown, sprinkling on the almonds for the last 5 minutes or so. Serve at once.

COOK'S TIP

Choux pastry is remarkably easy to make, as no rolling out is required. The secret of success is to let the flour and butter mixture cool before beating in the eggs, to prevent them from setting.

Cabbage Roulades with Lemon Sauce

Cabbage or chard leaves filled with a rice and lentil stuffing and served with a light egg lemon sauce makes a light and tasty main course.

SERVES 4–6
12 large cabbage or chard leaves, stalks removed
salt
2 tbsp sunflower oil
1 onion, chopped
1 large carrot, grated
4 oz sliced mushrooms
2½ cups stock
½ cup long grain rice
4 tbsp red lentils
1 tsp dried oregano or marjoram
ground black pepper
3½ oz soft cheese with garlic
SAUCE
3 tbsp all-purpose flour
juice of 1 lemon
3 eggs, beaten

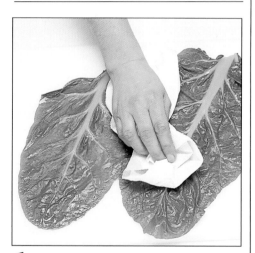

1 Blanch the leaves in boiling, salted water until they begin to wilt. Drain, reserve the water and pat the leaves dry with paper towel.

2 Heat the oil and lightly fry the onion, carrot and mushrooms for 5 minutes, and then pour in the stock.

3 Add the rice, lentils, herbs and seasoning. Bring to a boil, cover and simmer gently for 15 minutes. Remove from the heat, then stir in the cheese. Preheat the oven to 375°F.

4 Lay out the chard or cabbage leaves rib side down, and spoon on the filling at the stalk end. Fold the sides in and roll up.

5 Place the join side down in a small roasting pan and pour in the reserved cabbage water. Cover with lightly greased foil and bake for 30–45 minutes until the leaves are tender.

6 Remove the cabbage rolls from the oven, drain over a bowl and place on a serving dish. Strain 2½ cups of the cooking water into a saucepan and bring to a boil.

7 Blend the flour to a runny paste with a little cold water and whisk into the boiling stock, together with the lemon juice.

8 Beat the eggs in a heatproof bowl and slowly pour on the hot stock, whisking well as you go.

9 Return to the stove and on the lowest heat, stir until smooth and thick. Do not allow the sauce to boil or it will start to curdle. Serve the rolls with some of the sauce poured over and the rest passed round separately.

Irish Colcannon

This lovely warming winter dish bears a slight resemblance to Eggs Florentine. Here, baked eggs nestle among creamy potatoes with curly kale or cabbage and a topping of grated cheese.

SERVES 4
2 lb potatoes, cut in even pieces
8 oz curly kale or crisp green cabbage, shredded
2 scallions, chopped
butter or margarine, to taste
fresh nutmeg, grated
salt and ground black pepper
4 large eggs
3 oz aged cheese, grated

1 Boil the potatoes until just tender, then drain and mash well.

2 Lightly cook the kale or cabbage until just tender but still crisp. Preheat the oven to 375°F.

3 Drain the greens and mix them into the potato with the scallions, butter or margarine and nutmeg. Season to taste.

4 Spoon the mixture into a shallow ovenproof dish and make four hollows in the mixture. Break an egg into each and season well.

5 Bake for about 12 minutes or until the eggs are just set, then serve sprinkled with the cheese.

Pasta with Caponata

The Sicilians have an excellent sweet and sour vegetable dish called *caponata*, which naturally enough goes wonderfully well with pasta.

SERVES 4
1 medium eggplant, cut into sticks
2 medium zucchini, cut into sticks
8 baby onions, peeled or 1 large onion, sliced
2 garlic cloves, crushed
1 large red pepper, sliced
4 tbsp olive oil, preferably highly flavored extra virgin
scant 2 cups tomato juice or 1 × 17 fl oz carton puréed tomatoes
2/3 cup water
2 tbsp balsamic vinegar
juice of 1 lemon
1 tbsp sugar
2 tbsp sliced black olives
2 tbsp capers
salt and ground black pepper
14 oz tagliatelle or other long pasta ribbons

1 Lightly salt the eggplant and zucchini and leave them to drain in a colander for 30 minutes. Rinse thoroughly and pat dry with paper towel.

2 In a large saucepan, lightly fry the onions, garlic and pepper in the oil for 5 minutes, then stir in the eggplant and zucchini and fry for a further 5 minutes.

3 Stir in the tomato juice or puréed tomatoes, along with the water. Stir well, bringing the mixture to a boil, then add all the rest of the ingredients except the pasta. Season to taste and then simmer for 10 minutes.

4 Meanwhile, boil the pasta according to the instructions on the package, then drain. Serve the caponata with the pasta.

Spinach Gnocchi

This wholesome Italian dish is ideal for making in advance then baking when required. Serve it with a fresh tomato sauce.

SERVES 4–6
14 oz fresh leaf spinach, well washed, or 6 oz frozen leaf spinach, thawed
good 3 cups milk
1¼ cups semolina
4 tbsp butter, melted
2 oz Parmesan cheese, freshly grated, plus extra to serve
fresh nutmeg, grated
salt and ground black pepper
2 eggs, beaten

2 In a large saucepan, heat the milk and when just on the point of boiling, sprinkle in the semolina in a steady stream, stirring it briskly with a wooden spoon.

5 Stamp out shapes using a plain round cutter with a diameter of about 1½ in. Reserve the trimmings.

1 Blanch the spinach in the tiniest amount of water, then drain and squeeze dry through a sieve with the back of a ladle. Chop the spinach roughly.

3 Simmer the semolina for 2 minutes then remove from the heat and stir in half the butter, most of the cheese, nutmeg and seasoning to taste and the spinach. Allow to cool for 5 minutes.

6 Grease a shallow ovenproof dish. Place the trimmings on the base and arrange the gnocchi rounds on top with each one overlapping.

7 Brush the tops with the remaining butter and sprinkle over the last of the grated cheese.

8 Preheat the oven when ready to bake to 375°F and cook for about 35 minutes until golden and crisp on top. Serve hot with fresh tomato sauce and extra cheese.

VARIATION

For a special occasion, make half plain and half spinach gnocchi and arrange in an attractive pattern to serve. Use the same recipe as above but halve the amount of spinach and add to half the mixture in a separate bowl to make two batches. Stamp out and cook the gnocchi as normal. For a more substantial, healthy meal, make a tasty vegetable base of lightly sautéed peppers, zucchini and mushrooms and place the gnocchi on the top.

4 Stir in the eggs then tip the mixture out onto a shallow baking sheet, spreading it out to a ½ in thickness. Allow to cool completely, then chill until solid.

Red Rice Rissoles

Arborio rice chills to a firm texture, yet remains light and creamy when reheated as crisp crumbed rissoles. These contain small nuggets of cheese for extra creaminess.

SERVES ABOUT 8
1 large red onion, chopped
1 red pepper, chopped
2 garlic cloves, crushed
1 red chili, finely chopped
2 tbsp olive oil
2 tbsp butter
1¼ cups Arborio rice
4½ cups stock
4 sun-dried tomatoes, chopped
2 tbsp tomato paste
2 tsp dried oregano
salt and ground black pepper
3 tbsp fresh parsley, chopped
6 oz cheese, e.g. smoked Gouda or
   aged Cheddar
1 egg, beaten
1 cup dried bread crumbs
oil, for deep frying

1 Fry the onion, pepper, garlic and chili in the oil and butter for 5 minutes. Stir in the rice and fry for a further 2 minutes.

2 Pour in the stock and add the tomatoes, paste, oregano and seasoning. Bring to a boil, stirring occasionally, then cover and simmer for 20 minutes.

3 Stir in the parsley, then turn into a shallow dish and chill until firm. When cold, divide the mixture into 12 and shape into balls.

4 Cut the cheese into 12 pieces and press a nugget into the center of each of the rissoles.

5 Put the beaten egg in one bowl and the bread crumbs into another. Dip the rissoles first into the egg then into the bread crumbs, coating each one evenly.

6 Lay the coated rissoles on a plate and chill again for 30 minutes. Fill a deep fat frying pan one-third full of oil and heat until a cube of day-old bread browns in under a minute.

7 Fry the rissoles in batches, reheating the oil in between, for about 3–4 minutes. Drain on paper towel and keep warm, uncovered, before serving.

Broad Bean and Cauliflower Curry

A tasty mid-week curry to serve with rice (especially a brown basmati), small papadums and maybe a cool cucumber raita.

SERVES 4
2 garlic cloves, chopped
1 in cube fresh ginger root
1 fresh green chili, seeded and chopped
1 tbsp oil
1 onion, sliced
1 large potato, chopped
2 tbsp ghee or softened butter
1 tbsp curry powder, mild or hot
1 medium size cauliflower, cut into small florets
2½ cups stock
2 tbsp creamed coconut
salt and ground black pepper
1 × 10 oz can broad beans, with liquor
juice of half a lemon (optional)
fresh coriander or parsley, chopped, to serve

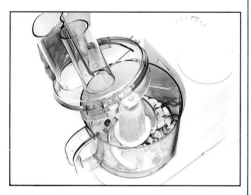

1 Blend the garlic, ginger, chili and oil in a food processor until they form a smooth paste.

2 In a large saucepan, fry the onion and potato in the ghee or butter for 5 minutes then stir in the spice paste and curry powder. Cook for 1 minute.

3 Add the cauliflower florets and stir well into the spicy mixture, then pour in the stock. Bring to a boil and mix in the coconut, stirring until it melts.

4 Season well, then cover and simmer for 10 minutes. Add the beans and their liquor and cook uncovered for a further 10 minutes.

5 Check the seasoning and add a good squeeze of lemon juice if liked. Serve hot garnished with coriander or parsley.

SALADS & VEGETABLE DISHES

Here is a delightful range of colorful salads and delicious vegetable dishes and accompaniments. Varied but easy to obtain ingredients ensure the perfect recipe for every style of meal.

Bean Sprout Stir-fry

Home grown bean sprouts taste so good, tossed into a tasty stir-fry. They have more flavor and texture than store-bought varieties and are very nutritious, being rich in vitamins and high in fiber. (Old dried beans will not sprout, so use beans that are well within their "Use by" date).

SERVES 3–4
2 tbsp sunflower or groundnut oil
8 oz mixed sprouted beans
2 scallions, chopped
1 garlic clove, crushed
2 tbsp soy sauce
2 tsp sesame oil
1 tbsp sesame seeds
2 tbsp fresh coriander or parsley, chopped
salt and ground black pepper

1 Heat the sunflower or groundnut oil in a large wok and stir-fry the sprouting beans, scallions and garlic for 5 minutes.

2 Add the remaining ingredients, cook for 1–2 minutes more and serve hot.

Panzanella Salad

If sliced juicy tomatoes layered with day old bread sounds strange for a salad, don't be deceived – it's quite delicious. A popular Italian salad, this dish is ideal as a starter or an accompaniment. Use full-flavored tomatoes for the best result.

SERVES 4–6
4 thick slices day-old bread, either white, brown or rye
1 small red onion, thinly sliced
1 lb ripe tomatoes, thinly sliced
4 oz Mozzarella cheese, thinly sliced
1 tbsp fresh basil, shredded, or marjoram
salt and ground black pepper
½ cup extra virgin olive oil
3 tbsp balsamic vinegar
juice of 1 small lemon
pitted and sliced black olives or salted capers, to garnish

1 Dip the bread briefly in cold water, then carefully squeeze out the excess water. Arrange on the bottom of a shallow salad bowl.

2 Soak the onion slices in cold water for about 10 minutes while you prepare the other ingredients. Drain and reserve.

3 Layer the tomatoes, cheese, onion and basil or marjoram, seasoning well in between each layer. Sprinkle with oil, vinegar and lemon juice.

4 Top with the olives or capers, cover with plastic wrap and then chill in the refrigerator overnight, if possible.

Caesar's Salad

On Independence Day 1924, in Tijuana, Mexico, a restauranteur – Caesar Cardini – created this masterpiece of new American cuisine. It has all the elements of a good salad – being light, flavorsome, attractive and nutritious with a good crunch.

SERVES 4
2 thick slices crustless bread
2 garlic cloves
sunflower oil, for frying
1 Romaine lettuce, washed and torn in pieces
½ cup fresh Parmesan cheese, coarsely grated
2 eggs
DRESSING
2 tbsp extra virgin olive oil
2 tsp French mustard
2 tsp Worcestershire sauce
2 tbsp fresh lemon juice

1 Cut the bread into cubes. Heat one of the garlic cloves slowly in about 3 tbsp of the sunflower oil in a saucepan and then toss in the bread cubes. Remove the garlic clove.

2 Heat the oven to 375°F. Spread the garlicky cubes on a baking sheet and bake the bread for about 10–12 minutes until golden and crisp. Remove and allow to cool completely.

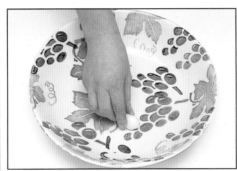

3 Rub the inside of a large salad bowl with the remaining garlic clove and then discard it.

4 Toss in the torn lettuce, sprinkling between the leaves with the cheese. Cover and set the salad aside.

5 Boil a small saucepan of water and cook the eggs for 1 minute only. Remove the eggs, and crack them open into a jug or bowl. The whites should be milky and the yolks raw.

6 Whisk the dressing ingredients into the eggs. When ready to serve pour the dressing over the leaves, toss well together and serve topped with the croûtons.

VARIATION

Why not try a refreshing Italian version of this salad? Use cubed ciabatta bread for the croûtons. Rub the inside of a salad bowl with garlic and spoon in 2–3 tbsp of good olive oil. Add a selection of torn salad leaves, including arugula, together with some shaved Parmesan cheese. Do not mix yet. Just before serving, add the croûtons, season well, then toss the leaves with the oil, coating well. Finally, squeeze over the juice of a fresh lemon.

Chef's Salad

This is basically whatever you make of it – a lovely large salad containing all your favourite ingredients. It is also a good opportunity to use up leftover vegetables and small pieces of cheese from the refrigerator. For these reasons, quantities are approximate.

SERVES 6

1 lb new potatoes, halved if large
2 carrots, coarsely grated
½ small fennel bulb or 2 stalks celery, sliced thinly
2 oz sliced button mushrooms
¼ cucumber, sliced or chopped
small green or red pepper, sliced
4 tbsp peas
1 cup cooked pulses, e.g. red kidney beans or green lentils
1 Boston or red leaf lettuce, or 1 head chicory
2–3 hard-boiled eggs, quartered, and/or grated cheese, to serve
small bunch watercress, snipped

1 Put all the vegetables and pulses (except the lettuce or chicory) into a large mixing bowl.

DRESSING
4 tbsp mayonnaise
3 tbsp natural yogurt
2 tbsp milk
2 tbsp chopped fresh chives or scallion tops
salt and ground black pepper

2 Line a large platter with the lettuce or chicory leaves – creating a nest for the other salad ingredients. Mix the dressing ingredients together and pour over the salad in the mixing bowl.

3 Toss the salad thoroughly in the dressing, season well then pile into the center of the lettuce or chicory nest.

4 Top the salad with the eggs, cheese or both and sprinkle with the snipped watercress. Serve lightly chilled.

Potato and Radish Salad 🍃

So many potato salads are dressed in thick sauce. This one is quite light and colorful with a flavorsome yet delicate dressing.

SERVES 4–6
1 lb new potatoes, scrubbed
3 tbsp olive oil
1 tbsp walnut or hazelnut oil (optional)
2 tbsp wine vinegar
2 tsp coarse grain mustard
1 tsp honey
salt and ground black pepper
about 6–8 radishes, thinly sliced
2 tbsp fresh chives, chopped

1 Boil the potatoes until just tender. Drain, return to the pan and cut any large potatoes in half.

2 Make a dressing with the oils, vinegar, mustard, honey and seasoning. Mix them together thoroughly in a bowl.

3 Toss the dressing into the potatoes while they are still cooling and allow them to stand for an hour or so.

4 Mix in the radishes and chives, chill lightly, toss again and serve.

COOK'S TIP

The secret of a good potato salad is to dress the potatoes while still warm in a vinaigrette-style dressing in order to let them soak up the flavor as they cool. You can then mix in an additional creamy dressing of mayonnaise and natural yogurt if liked. Sliced celery, red onion and chopped walnuts would make a good alternative to the radishes and, for best effect, serve on a platter lined with frilly lettuce leaves.

Thai Rice and Sprouting Beans

Thai rice has a delicate fragrance and texture that is delicious whether served hot or cold. This salad is a colorful collection of popular Thai flavors and textures.

SERVES 6
2 tbsp sesame oil
2 tbsp fresh lime juice
1 small fresh red chili, seeded and
  chopped
1 garlic clove, crushed
2 tsp fresh ginger root, grated
2 tbsp light soy sauce
1 tsp honey
3 tbsp pineapple juice
1 tbsp wine vinegar
1¼ cups Thai fragrant rice, boiled
2 scallions, sliced
2 rings canned pineapple in natural juice,
  chopped
1¼ cups sprouted lentils or bean sprouts
1 small red pepper, sliced
1 stalk celery, sliced
½ cup unsalted cashew nuts, roughly
  chopped
2 tbsp toasted sesame seeds
salt and ground black pepper

1 Whisk together the sesame oil, lime juice, chili, garlic, ginger, soy sauce, honey, pineapple juice and vinegar in a large bowl. Stir in the lightly boiled rice.

2 Toss in all the remaining ingredients and mix well. This dish can be served warm or lightly chilled. If the rice grains stick together on cooling, simply stir them with a metal spoon.

Chicory, Carrot and Arugula Salad

A bright and colorful salad which is ideal for a buffet or barbecue party. Use watercress if you are unable to obtain any arugula.

SERVES 4–6
3 carrots, coarsely grated
about 2 oz fresh arugula or watercress,
  roughly chopped
1 large head chicory
DRESSING:
3 tbsp sunflower oil
1 tbsp hazelnut or walnut oil (optional)
2 tbsp cider or wine vinegar
2 tsp honey
1 tsp grated lemon rind
1 tbsp poppy seeds
salt and ground black pepper

1 Mix the carrot and arugula or watercress together in a large bowl and season well.

2 Shake the dressing ingredients together in a screw top jar then pour onto the carrot and greenery. Toss the salad thoroughly.

3 Line a shallow salad bowl with the chicory leaves and spoon the salad into the centre. Serve lightly chilled.

Bountiful Bean and Nut Salad

This is a good multi-purpose dish. It can be a cold main course, a buffet party dish, or a salad on the side. It also keeps well for up to three days in the refrigerator.

SERVES 6
½ cup red kidney, pinto or borlotti beans
½ cup white cannellini or lima beans
2 tbsp olive oil
6 oz cut fresh green beans
3 scallions, sliced
1 small yellow or red pepper, sliced
1 carrot, coarsely grated
2 tbsp dried onion flakes or sun-dried
　tomatoes, chopped
½ cup unsalted cashew nuts or almonds,
　split in half
DRESSING
3 tbsp sunflower oil
2 tbsp red wine vinegar
1 tbsp coarse grain mustard
1 tsp superfine sugar
1 tsp dried mixed herbs
salt and ground black pepper

1 Soak the beans, overnight if possible, then drain and rinse well, cover with a lot of cold water and cook according to the instructions on the package.

2 When cooked, drain and season the beans and toss them in the olive oil. Leave to cool for 30 minutes.

3 In a large bowl, mix in the other vegetables, including the sun-dried tomatoes but not the dried onion flakes, if using, or the nuts.

4 Make up the dressing by shaking all the ingredients together in a screw top jar. Toss the dressing into the salad and check the seasoning again. Serve sprinkled with the onion flakes, if using, and the split nuts.

Garden Salad and Garlic Crostini

Dress a colorful mixture of salad leaves with good olive oil and freshly squeezed lemon juice, then top it with crispy bread crostini.

SERVES 4—6
3 thick slices day old bread, e.g. ciabatta
½ cup extra virgin olive oil
garlic clove, cut
½ small Boston or Romaine lettuce
½ small oak leaf lettuce
1 oz arugula leaves or watercress
1 oz fresh flat leaf parsley
a few leaves and flowers of nasturtium
a small handful of young dandelion
  leaves
sea salt flakes and ground black pepper
juice of 1 fresh lemon

1 Cut the bread into medium size dice about ½ in square.

2 Heat half the oil gently in a frying pan and fry the bread cubes in it, tossing them until they are well coated and lightly browned. Remove and cool.

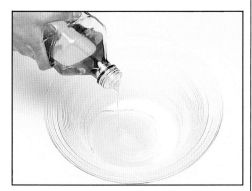

3 Rub the inside of a large salad bowl with the garlic and discard. Pour the rest of the oil into the bottom of the bowl.

4 Wash, dry and tear the leaves into bite size pieces and pile them into the bowl. Season with salt and pepper. Cover and keep chilled until ready to serve.

5 To serve, toss the leaves in the oil at the bottom of the bowl, then sprinkle with the lemon juice and toss again. Scatter over the crostini and serve immediately.

Californian Salad

Full of vitality and vitamins, this is a lovely light healthy salad for sunny days when you need an extra boost.

SERVES 4
1 small crisp lettuce, torn in pieces
8 oz young spinach leaves, well washed
2 carrots, coarsely grated
4 oz cherry tomatoes, halved
2 celery stalks, thinly sliced
½ cup raisins
½ cup blanched almonds or unsalted
  cashew nuts, halved
2 tbsp sunflower seeds
2 tbsp sesame seeds, lightly toasted
DRESSING:
3 tbsp extra virgin olive oil
2 tbsp cider vinegar
2 tsp honey
juice of 1 small orange
salt and ground black pepper

1 Put the salad vegetables, raisins, almonds or cashew nuts and seeds into a large bowl.

2 Put all the dressing ingredients into a screw top jar, shake them up well and pour over the salad.

3 Toss the salad thoroughly and divide it between four small salad bowls. Season and serve lightly chilled.

Scandinavian Cucumber and Dill

It's amazing what a light touch of salt can do to simple cucumber slices. They take on a contradictory soft yet crisp texture and develop a good, full flavor. However, juices continue to form after salting, so this salad is best dressed just before serving. It is particularly complementary to hot and spicy food.

SERVES 4
2 cucumbers
salt
2 tbsp fresh chives, chopped
2 tbsp fresh dill, chopped
⅔ cup sour cream or natural yogurt
ground black pepper

1 Slice the cucumbers as thinly as possible, preferably in a food processor or a slicer.

2 Place the slices in layers in a colander set over a plate to catch the juices. Sprinkling each layer well, but not too heavily, with salt.

3 Leave the cucumber to drain for up to 2 hours, then lay out the slices on a clean dish towel and pat them dry.

4 Mix the cucumber with the herbs, cream or yogurt and plenty of pepper. Serve as soon as possible.

COOK'S TIP

Deseeded and lightly salted cucumbers are also delicious as sandwich fillings in wafer thin buttered brown bread. These sandwiches were always served at traditional tea parties.

Spinach Roulade

A simple purée of spinach baked with eggs rolled around a creamy red pepper filling makes an exotic and colorful side dish. Even better, this can be prepared in advance and then reheated when required.

SERVES 4
1 lb leaf spinach, well washed and
  drained
fresh nutmeg, grated
2 tbsp butter, softened
3 tbsp Parmesan cheese, grated
3 tbsp heavy cream
salt and ground black pepper
2 eggs, separated
1 small red pepper, chopped
7 oz soft cheese with garlic and herbs

1 Line a medium size jelly roll pan with waxed paper and grease the paper. Preheat the oven to 375°F.

2 Cook the spinach with a tiny amount of water then drain well, pressing it through a sieve with the back of a ladle. Chop the spinach finely.

3 Mix the spinach with the nutmeg, butter, Parmesan cheese, cream and seasoning. Cool for 5 minutes, then beat in the egg yolks.

4 Whisk the egg whites until they form soft peaks and carefully fold in to the spinach mixture. Spread in to the prepared pan, level and bake for 12–15 minutes until firm.

5 Turn the spinach out upside down on to a clean dish towel and allow it to cool in the pan for half an hour.

6 Meanwhile, simmer the pepper in about 2 tbsp of water in a covered pan until just soft, then either purée it in a blender or chop it finely. Mix with the soft cheese and season well.

7 When the spinach has cooled, peel off the paper. Trim any hard edges and spread it with the red pepper cream.

8 Carefully roll up the spinach and pepper in the dish towel, leave for 10 minutes to firm up, then serve on a long platter, cut in thick slices.

VARIATION

A thick vegetable purée of any root vegetable also works well as a roulade. Try cooked beets or parsnip, flavoring lightly with a mild curry-style spice such as cumin or coriander. The fillings can be varied too, such as finely chopped and sautéed mushroom and onion, or grated carrot mixed with yogurt and chives. Roulades are delicious served warm as well. Sprinkle with cheese and bake in a moderately hot oven for 15 minutes or so.

Indian Spiced Okra with Almonds

Long and elegantly shaped, it is not surprising these vegetables have the popular name of "lady's fingers." Although commonly used in many international dishes, okra are particularly well suited to all the Indian spices.

SERVES 2—4
8 oz okra
½ cup blanched almonds, chopped
2 tbsp butter
1 tbsp sunflower oil
2 garlic cloves, crushed
1 in cube fresh ginger root, grated
1 tsp cumin seeds
1 tsp ground coriander
1 tsp paprika

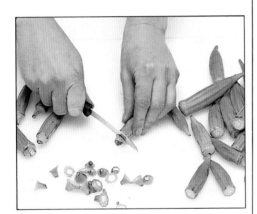

1 Trim just the tops of the okra stems and around the edges of the stalks. They have a sticky liquid which oozes out if prepared too far ahead, so trim them immediately before cooking.

2 In a shallow fireproof dish, fry the almonds in the butter until they are lightly golden, then remove.

3 Add the oil to the pan and fry the okra, stirring constantly, for 2 minutes.

4 Add the garlic and ginger and fry gently for a minute, then add the spices and cook for another minute or so, stirring all the time.

VARIATION

Okra are also popular in Louisiana cooking and are an essential ingredient for gumbo, a thick, spicy stew served over hot, steaming rice. Indeed, 'gumbo' was the old African word for okra used by the American slaves. You can make a ratatouille-style vegetable stew using okra instead of eggplant, and adding onions, peppers, garlic and tomatoes. Or try them sliced, fried in garlic and spices, then stirred into a pilaf of basmati rice with cauliflower florets and carrots. This makes a colorful and delicious dish – especially when topped with crushed grilled papadums.

5 Pour in approximately 1¼ cups of water. Season well, cover and simmer for about 5 minutes or so until the okra feel just tender.

6 Finally, mix in the fried almonds and serve piping hot.

Roasted Peppers in Oil 🍃

Peppers take on a delicious, smokey flavor if roasted in a very hot oven. The skins can easily be peeled off and the flesh stored in olive oil. This oil can then be used to add extra flavor to salad dressings.

6 large peppers of differing colors
scant 2 cups olive oil

1 Preheat the oven to the highest temperature, about 450°F. Lightly grease a large baking sheet.

2 Quarter the peppers, remove the cores and seeds then squash them flat with the back of your hands. Lay the peppers skin side up on the baking tray.

3 Roast the peppers at the top of the oven until the skins blacken and blister. This will take about 12–15 minutes.

4 Remove the peppers from the oven, cover with a clean dish towel until they are cool, then peel off the skins.

5 Slice the peppers and pack them into a clean preserving jar.

COOK'S TIP

These pepper slices make very attractive presents, especially around Christmas time. You can either buy special preserving jars from kitchen equipment shops, or wash out large jam jars, soaking off the labels at the same time. The jars should then be sterilized by placing upside down in a low oven for about half an hour. Fill the jars while still hot with the sliced peppers, and fill with a good olive oil. Cover immediately with the lid and fix on an attractive label.

6 Add the oil to the jar to cover the peppers completely, then seal the lid.

7 Store the peppers in the refrigerator and use them within 2 weeks. Use the oil in dressing or for cooking once the peppers have been eaten.

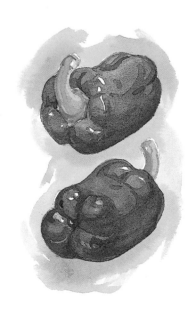

Potato Latkes

These little potato pancakes make a pleasant and unusual alternative to chips or roast potatoes.

MAKES ABOUT 24
2 lb potatoes, peeled and coarsely grated
scant ½ cup self-rising flour
2 eggs
1 tbsp onion, grated
fresh nutmeg, grated
salt and ground black pepper
oil, for shallow frying

1 Soak the grated potato in plenty of cold water for about an hour, then drain well and pat dry with a clean dish towel.

2 Beat together the flour, eggs, onion and nutmeg, then mix in the potato. Season well.

3 Heat a thin layer of oil in a heavy based frying pan and drop about a tablespoon of potato batter into the pan, squashing it flat, if necessary.

4 Cook the potato until golden brown, then flip over and cook the other side. Drain on paper towel and keep warm, uncovered, in the oven. Repeat with the rest of the mixture.

Stir-fried Eggplant

A speedy side dish with an Oriental touch. The eggplant is stir-fried with red pepper and black beans which give it a really exotic and colorful appearance. Salted black beans are sold either dried or canned. Dried ones will need soaking.

SERVES 4
2 tbsp groundnut oil
1 eggplant, sliced
2 scallions, sliced diagonally
1 garlic clove, crushed
1 small red pepper, sliced
2 tbsp oyster sauce
1 tbsp Chinese salted black beans, soaked
  if dried
ground black pepper
1 tbsp fresh coriander or parsley,
  chopped, to garnish

1 Heat the oil in a wok and stir-fry the eggplant for 2 minutes. Add the scallions, garlic and pepper and cook for a further 2 minutes.

2 Add the oyster sauce, black beans and pepper. Cook for a further minute, season with pepper only and serve with fresh coriander or parsley.

Potato and Parsnip Dauphinoise

Layers of potatoes and parsnips are baked slowly in creamy milk with grated cheese. This is an ideal special side dish or light supper dish.

SERVES 4–6
2 lb potatoes, thinly sliced
1 onion, thinly sliced
1 lb parsnips, thinly sliced
2 garlic cloves, crushed
4 tbsp butter
4 oz Gruyère or Cheddar cheese, grated
fresh nutmeg, grated
salt and ground black pepper
1¼ cups light cream
1¼ cups milk

1 Lightly grease a large shallow ovenproof dish, and then preheat the oven to 350°F.

2 Layer the potatoes with the onion and parsnips. In between each layer, dot the vegetables with garlic and butter, sprinkle over most of the cheese, add the nutmeg and season well.

3 Heat the cream and milk together in a saucepan until they are hot but not boiling. Slowly pour the creamy milk over the vegetables, making sure it seeps underneath them.

4 Scatter the remaining cheese over the vegetables and grate a little more nutmeg on top. Bake for about an hour or so until the potatoes are tender and the cheese top is bubbling and golden.

Asparagus Mimosa

Pretty spears of fresh, tender asparagus are tossed in a buttery sauce and served with a chopped egg and chervil dressing. This also makes an excellent starter.

SERVES 2
8 oz fresh asparagus
salt
ground black pepper
4 tbsp butter, melted
squeeze of fresh lemon juice
2 eggs, hard-boiled and chopped
1 tbsp fresh chervil, chopped

1 Trim the asparagus stalks and peel off the tough outer layers at the base with a vegetable peeler.

2 Poach the asparagus spears in lightly salted water, until just tender. This will take between 3–6 minutes. (Use a clean, deep frying pan if you don't have an asparagus steamer.)

3 Drain the asparagus well and arrange it on two small plates or one large one. Season well.

4 Mix the melted butter with the lemon juice. Trickle over the spears, sprinkle with the eggs and garnish with the chervil. Serve warm.

Braised Fennel and Tomato

Fennel is a very undervalued vegetable but it is excellent cooked in a light tomato sauce. This dish can be gently simmered on the stove or baked in a moderate oven.

SERVES 4–6
2 fennel bulbs
1 small onion or 3 shallots, sliced
1 garlic clove, crushed
2 tbsp olive oil
4 medium sized tomatoes, peeled and chopped
3 tbsp dry white wine
1 tbsp fresh marjoram, chopped
⅔ cup stock or water
salt and ground black pepper

1 Trim the fennel and then cut it into wedges. Reserve any fronds for a garnish.

2 Lightly sauté the fennel with the onion or shallots and garlic in the oil in a fireproof dish for 5 minutes.

3 Add the tomatoes, wine, marjoram and stock or water. Season.

4 Cover and either simmer very gently for 20 minutes, or bake in a preheated oven for 30 minutes at 375°F. Garnish with any reserved fronds of fennel and serve immediately.

Creamed Winter Vegetables

A mixture of chunky mashed root vegetables, such as carrots, parsnips and rutabaga, makes a wonderfully warming winter side dish.

SERVES 4–6
8 oz carrots, chopped
8 oz parsnips, chopped
1 small rutabaga, chopped
2 tbsp butter
2 tsp mild curry paste
salt and ground black pepper
½ cup ricotta cheese
1 tbsp fresh chives, chopped

1 Boil the carrots, parsnips and rutabaga in plenty of lightly salted water until tender. Drain the vegetables, then return them to the pan with the butter, curry paste and seasoning.

2 Mash the vegetables lightly with a fork so that you end up with a chunky purée; you want to retain a good texture.

3 Stir in the ricotta cheese and chives. Check the seasoning and serve hot. This is a good dish to prepare in advance and reheat when required.

COOK'S TIP

Vegetable purées are a popular accompaniment with any dish which could be a little on the dry side, providing a good contrast of textures and colors. Suitable vegetables are Brussels sprouts, carrots, peas, broccoli and leeks.

PARTIES
&
PICNICS

From informal meals, ideal for outdoor entertaining, to elegant and delicious dishes that will add style to special occasions, here are recipes to suit every festivity.

Spicy Potato Strudel

Wrap up a tasty mixture of vegetables in a spicy, creamy sauce with crisp filo pastry. It makes a perfect dish for a special family supper.

SERVES 4
1 onion, chopped
2 carrots, coarsely grated
1 zucchini, chopped
12 oz potatoes, chopped
5 tbsp butter
2 tsp mild curry paste
½ tsp dried thyme
⅔ cup water
salt and ground black pepper
1 egg, beaten
2 tbsp light cream
½ cup Cheddar cheese, grated
8 sheets filo pastry
sesame seeds, to sprinkle

1 Fry the onion, carrots, zucchini and potatoes in half the butter for 5 minutes until they are soft, then add the curry paste and cook for a further minute.

2 Add the thyme, water and seasoning. Continue to cook gently, uncovered for another 10 minutes.

3 Allow the mixture to cool and mix in the egg, cream and cheese. Chill until ready to fill and roll.

4 Melt the remaining butter and lay out four sheets of filo pastry, slightly overlapping them to form a fairly large rectangle. Brush with butter and fit the other sheets on top. Brush again.

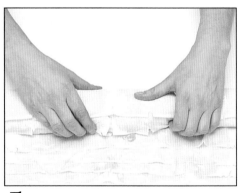

5 Spoon the filling along one long edge, then roll up the pastry. Form it into a circle and brush again with the last of the butter. Sprinkle over the sesame seeds and set on a baking sheet.

6 Heat the oven to 375°F, then bake the strudel for about 25 minutes until golden and crisp. Allow to stand for 5 minutes or so before cutting.

Coronation Salad

This famous salad dressing was created especially for the coronation dinner of Queen Elizabeth II. It is a wonderful accompaniment to eggs and vegetables.

SERVES 6
1 lb new potatoes
salt
3 tbsp vinaigrette dressing
3 scallions, chopped
ground black pepper
6 eggs, hard-boiled and halved
frilly lettuce leaves, to serve
¼ cucumber, sliced then cut in shreds
6 large radishes, sliced
1 bunch watercress
DRESSING
2 tbsp olive oil
1 small onion, chopped
1 tbsp mild curry powder or korma
  spice mix
2 tsp tomato paste
2 tbsp lemon juice
2 tbsp sherry
1¼ cups mayonnaise
¼ pint natural yogurt

1 Boil the potatoes in salted water until tender. Drain them and then toss them in the vinaigrette dressing.

2 Allow the potatoes to cool, stirring in the scallions and seasoning. Cool the mixture thoroughly.

3 Meanwhile, make the coronation dressing. Heat the oil and fry the onion for 3 minutes until it is soft. Stir in the spice powder and fry for a further minute. Mix in all the other dressing ingredients.

4 Stir the dressing into the potatoes, add the eggs then chill. Line a serving platter with lettuce leaves and pile the salad in the center. Scatter over the cucumber, radishes and watercress.

Pasta and Wild Mushroom Casserole

Bake pasta shapes in a golden crumb coating layered with a rich bechamel sauce and mushrooms. Superb!

SERVES 4–6
7 oz pasta shapes
2½ cups milk
1 bay leaf
small onion stuck with 6 cloves
4 tbsp butter
3 tbsp fresh bread crumbs
2 tsp dried mixed herbs
⅓ cup all-purpose flour
4 tbsp Parmesan cheese, freshly grated
fresh nutmeg, grated
salt and ground black pepper
2 eggs, beaten
1 × ½ oz package dried porcini or cep mushrooms
12 oz button mushrooms, sliced
2 garlic cloves, crushed
2 tbsp olive oil
2 tbsp fresh parsley, chopped

1 Boil the pasta according to the instructions on the package. Drain and set aside. Heat the milk with the bay leaf and clove-studded onion and stand for 15 minutes. Remove the bay leaf and onion.

2 Melt the butter in a saucepan and use a little to brush the inside of a large oval casserole. Mix the crumbs and mixed herbs together and use them to coat the inside of the dish.

3 Stir the flour into the butter, cook for a minute then slowly add the hot milk to make a smooth sauce. Add the cheese, nutmeg, seasoning and cooked pasta. Cool for 5 minutes then beat in the eggs.

4 Soak the porcini or cep mushrooms in a little hot water until soft. Reserve the liquor and chop the mushrooms.

5 Fry the porcinis or ceps with the button mushrooms and garlic in the oil for 3 minutes. Season, stir in the liquor and reduce down. Add the parsley.

6 Spoon a layer of pasta into the dish. Sprinkle over the mushrooms then more pasta and so on, finishing with pasta. Cover with greased foil. Heat the oven to 375°F and bake for about 25–30 minutes. Allow to stand for 5 minutes before turning out to serve.

Eggplant Boats

These can be prepared ahead and baked prior to eating. The hazelnut topping contrasts nicely with the smooth eggplant filling.

SERVES 4
⅔ cup brown basmati rice
2 medium size eggplants, halved lengthwise
1 onion, chopped
2 garlic cloves, crushed
1 small green pepper, chopped
4 oz mushrooms, sliced
3 tbsp olive oil
3 oz Cheddar cheese, grated
1 egg, beaten
½ tsp marjoram
salt and ground black pepper
2 tbsp hazelnuts, chopped

1 Boil the rice according to the instructions on the package, drain and then cool. Scoop out the flesh from the eggplants and chop. Blanch the shells in boiling water for 2 minutes, then drain upside down.

2 Fry the eggplant flesh, onion, garlic, pepper and mushrooms in the oil, for about 5 minutes.

3 Mix in the rice, cheese, egg, marjoram and seasoning. Arrange the eggplant shells in an ovenproof dish. Spoon the filling inside. Sprinkle over the nuts. Chill until ready to bake.

4 Heat the oven to 375°F and bake the eggplants for about 25 minutes until the filling is set and the nuts are golden brown in color.

Crêpe Galette

Make a stack of light crêpes and then layer them together with a tasty lentil filling for an impressive dinner party main course. Serve with a home made tomato sauce.

SERVES 6
1 cup all-purpose flour
good pinch of salt
1 egg
1¼ cups buttermilk, or milk and
   water, mixed
oil, for cooking
FILLING
2 leeks, thinly sliced
1 small fennel bulb, thinly sliced
4 tbsp olive oil
¾ cup red lentils
⅔ cup dry white wine
1 × 14 oz can chopped tomatoes
1¼ cups stock
1 tsp dried oregano
salt and ground black pepper
1 onion, sliced
8 oz mushrooms, sliced
8 oz frozen leaf spinach, thawed and
   squeezed dry
7 oz low fat cream cheese
2 oz Parmesan cheese, freshly grated

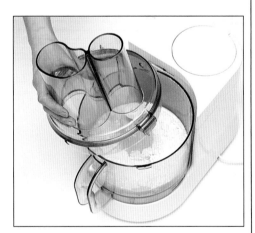

1 Make the crêpe batter by mixing the flour, salt, egg and buttermilk or milk and water in a blender until smooth. Set aside while you prepare the filling.

2 Gently fry the leeks and fennel in half the olive oil for 5 minutes, then add the lentils and wine. Cook for a minute until reduced down, then stir in the tomatoes and stock.

3 Bring the leek/fennel mixture to a boil, add the oregano and seasoning then simmer for 20 minutes, stirring it occasionally until it thickens.

4 Fry the onion and mushrooms in the remaining olive oil for 5 minutes, stir in the spinach and heat. Season well, then mix in the cream cheese.

5 Make about 12–14 crêpes with the batter in a well heated non-stick frying pan. Lightly grease an 8 in round deep spring-form cake pan and line the base and sides with some of the crêpes, overlapping them as necessary.

6 Layer the remaining crêpes with the two fillings, sprinkling Parmesan in between and pressing them down well. Finish with a crêpe on top.

7 Cover with foil and set aside to rest. Preheat the oven to 375°F. Bake for about 40 minutes, then turn out carefully and allow to firm up for 10 minutes before cutting into wedges.

COOK'S TIP

This can be frozen ready made up, but it is probably nicer if frozen in parts – the crêpes interleaved with waxed paper and then wrapped in foil, and the sauce frozen separately.

Polenta Fingers with Beans and Tomatoes

Polenta, or cornmeal, is a popular family favorite in Italy. It is eaten either hot from a bowl or allowed to set, cut into fingers, and grilled.

SERVES 6
7½ cups milk and water, mixed
2 tsp salt
1½ cups polenta
2 tbsp butter, plus extra for spreading
2 oz Parmesan cheese, freshly grated
ground black pepper
SAUCE
1 onion, chopped
2 garlic cloves, crushed
2 tbsp olive oil
1 × 14 oz can chopped tomatoes
salt and ground black pepper
good pinch of dried sage
8 oz frozen broad beans

1 In a large saucepan, bring the milk and water to a boil. Stir in the salt. While stirring with a wooden spoon trickle the polenta into the boiling liquid in a steady stream and continue stirring until the mixture has thickened.

2 Lower the heat and simmer for about 20 minutes, stirring frequently. Add the butter, cheese and seasoning.

3 Lightly grease a shallow roasting pan and pour in the polenta mixture. Cool, then chill overnight.

4 For the sauce, fry the onion and garlic in the oil for 5 minutes. Add the tomatoes, seasoning and sage and cook for a further 10 minutes. Stir in the broad beans and cook for 5 minutes more.

5 Turn out the polenta and cut into fingers. Grill both sides until brown and crisp. Spread with a little butter and serve accompanied by the tomato and beans.

Paprika and Parmesan Tartlets

Pretty pink pastry tarts with a tangy cream filling are ideal for handing round at cocktail parties. Make the shells ahead of the party and fill them just before serving.

MAKES 18
2 cups all-purpose flour
2 tsp paprika
10 tbsp butter or sunflower margarine
scant ½ cup Parmesan cheese, freshly grated
cold water, to bind
FILLING
12 oz goat cheese
2 oz arugula leaves, or watercress, chopped
2 tbsp fresh chives, chopped
salt and ground black pepper
1 lb tomatoes, sliced

1 Sift the flour with the paprika and rub in the butter or margarine. Stir in the Parmesan and mix to a firm dough with cold water.

2 Roll out the pastry and stamp out 18 rounds, large enough to fit into muffin pans. Prick the bases well with a fork, press them into the muffin pans and chill while you preheat the oven to 375°F.

3 Bake the tartlets for 15 minutes until crisp. Cool them on a wire rack.

4 Beat the cheese with the arugula or watercress, chives and seasoning. Slice the tomatoes, allowing roughly two slices per tart.

5 When ready to serve, spoon the filling into the tarts. Top each one with some tomato and garnish with extra arugula or watercress leaves.

Basmati and Green Lentil Salad

Puy lentils from France (sometimes known as green lentils) are small, deliciously nutty pulses, highly prized by gourmets. They blend beautifully with aromatic basmati rice.

SERVES 6
⅔ cup puys de dome (green) lentils, soaked
1¼ cups basmati rice, rinsed well
2 carrots, coarsely grated
⅓ cucumber, halved, seeded and coarsely grated
3 scallions, sliced
3 tbsp fresh parsley, chopped
DRESSING
2 tbsp sunflower oil
2 tbsp extra virgin olive oil
2 tbsp wine vinegar
2 tbsp fresh lemon juice
good pinch of granulated sugar
salt and ground black pepper

1 Soak the lentils for 30 minutes. Meanwhile, make the dressing by shaking all the ingredients together in a screw-topped jar. Set aside.

2 Boil the lentils in plenty of unsalted water for 20–25 minutes or until soft. Drain thoroughly.

3 Boil the basmati rice for 10 minutes, then drain.

4 Mix together the rice and lentils in the dressing and season well. Leave to cool.

5 Add the carrots, cucumber, scallions and parsley. Spoon into an attractive serving bowl and chill before serving.

Wild Rice with Julienne Vegetables

Make an accompanying dish more interesting with some exquisite wild rice. For the best flavor, buy a good quality wild rice (which is actually a cereal!) and, to shorten the cooking time, soak it overnight.

SERVES 4
½ cup wild rice
1 red onion, sliced
2 carrots, cut in julienne sticks
2 celery stalks, cut in julienne sticks
4 tbsp butter
⅔ cup stock or water
salt and ground black pepper
2 medium zucchini, cut in thicker sticks
a few toasted almond flakes, to serve

1 Drain the soaked rice, then boil in plenty of unsalted water for 15–20 minutes, until it is soft and many of the grains have burst open. Drain.

2 In another saucepan, gently fry the onion, carrots and celery in the butter for 2 minutes, then pour in the stock or water and season well.

3 Bring to a boil, simmer for 2 minutes then stir in the zucchini. Cook for 1 more minute then mix in the rice. Reheat and serve hot sprinkled with the almonds.

Oven-Crisp Asparagus Rolls

A lovely treat when fresh asparagus is in season is to wrap blanched spears in slices of thin bread and bake in a buttery glaze until crisp. Out of season, use canned or frozen spears.

SERVES 8
8 thick spears of fresh asparagus
salt
8½ tbsp butter, softened
1 tbsp coarse grained mustard
grated rind of 1 lemon
ground black pepper
8 slices thin white bread, crusts removed

1 Trim the asparagus stalks, peeling the tough woody skin at the base. Blanch until just tender in a shallow pan of boiling, salted water. Drain and refresh in cold water. Pat dry.

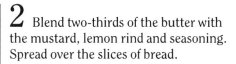

2 Blend two-thirds of the butter with the mustard, lemon rind and seasoning. Spread over the slices of bread.

3 Lay an asparagus spear on the edge of each bread slice and roll it up tightly. Place the rolls join side down on a lightly greased baking sheet.

4 Melt the remaining butter and brush over the rolls. Heat the oven to 375°F and bake for 12–15 minutes until golden and crisp. Cool slightly before serving.

VARIATION

Asparagus has always been something of a luxury as its season is so short, but imports from across the world means that it is available almost all year round, albeit at a price!

Thin baby asparagus, known as sprue, can be eaten raw in salads or stir-fried quickly. Opinions differ about the merits of green or white asparagus spears. The latter are forced in the dark (hence their white color), but some people consider them to have a better flavor and texture.

Ratatouille Tart

Serve this pretty tart warm so the cheese is easy to cut and eat. For the best results, make the base and filling separately then combine and heat just before serving.

SERVES 6
1 cup all-purpose flour
¾ cup whole wheat flour
1 tsp dried mixed herbs
salt and ground black pepper
½ cup sunflower margarine
3–4 tbsp cold water
FILLING
1 small eggplant, thickly sliced
salt
3 tbsp olive oil
1 onion, sliced
1 red or yellow pepper, sliced
2 garlic cloves, crushed
2 zucchini, thickly sliced
2 tomatoes, skinned and sliced
ground black pepper
2 tbsp fresh basil, chopped
5 oz Mozzarella cheese, sliced
2 tbsp pine nuts

1 Mix the two flours with the herbs and seasoning then rub in the margarine until it resembles fine crumbs. Mix to a firm dough with water.

2 Roll out the pastry and line a 9 in round pie pan. Prick the base, line with foil and baking beans then allow to rest in the fridge.

3 Meanwhile, sprinkle the eggplant lightly with salt and leave to drain for 30 minutes in a colander. Rinse and pat dry.

4 Heat the oil in a frying pan and fry the onion and pepper for 5 minutes, then add the garlic, zucchini and eggplant. Fry for a further 10 minutes, stirring the mixture occasionally.

5 Stir in the tomatoes and seasoning, cook for a further 3 minutes, add the basil then remove the pan from the heat and allow to cool.

6 Heat the oven to 400°F. Place the tart shell on a baking sheet and bake for 25 minutes, removing the foil and baking beans for the last 5 minutes. Cool and then, if possible, carefully remove the case from the pan.

7 When ready to serve, spoon the vegetables into the case using a slotted spoon so any juices drain off and don't soak into the pastry. Top with the cheese slices and pine nuts. Toast under a preheated broiler until golden and bubbling. Serve warm.

Filo Baskets with Ginger Dill Vegetables

Make up some elegant filo baskets, then fill them with crisply steamed vegetables tossed in an interesting and tasty sauce.

SERVES 4
4 sheets of filo pastry
3 tbsp butter, melted
FILLING
2 tbsp olive oil
1 tbsp fresh root ginger, grated
2 garlic cloves, crushed
3 shallots, sliced
8 oz wild mushrooms, sliced
4 oz oyster mushrooms, sliced
1 zucchini, sliced
7 oz sour cream
2 tbsp fresh dill, chopped
salt and ground black pepper
dill and parsley sprigs, to serve

1 Cut the filo sheets into four. Line four large muffin pans, angling the layers so that the corners form a pretty star shape. Brush between each layer with butter. Set aside.

2 Heat the oven to 375°F. Bake the shells for about 10 minutes until golden brown and crisp. Remove and cool.

3 For the filling, heat the oil and sauté the ginger, garlic and shallots for 2 minutes, then add the mushrooms and zucchini. Cook for another 3 minutes.

4 Mix in the sour cream, chopped dill and seasoning. Heat until just bubbling then spoon into the filo cases. Garnish with the dill and parsley and serve.

Gado Gado Salad with Peanut Sambal

Indonesians enjoy a salad of lightly steamed vegetables topped with a peanut sauce. It is ideal for a colorful summer buffet dish.

SERVES 6
8 oz new potatoes, halved
2 carrots, cut in sticks
4 oz green beans
½ small cauliflower, broken into florets
¼ firm white cabbage, shredded
7 oz bean or lentil sprouts
4 eggs, hard-boiled and quartered
bunch watercress, trimmed
SAUCE
6 tbsp crunchy peanut butter
1¼ cups cold water
1 garlic clove, crushed
2 tbsp dark soy sauce
1 tbsp dry sherry
2 tsp superfine sugar
1 tbsp fresh lemon juice
1 tsp anchovy paste

1 Fit a steamer or metal colander over a pan of gently boiling water. Cook the potatoes for 10 minutes.

2 Add the rest of the vegetables and sprouts and steam for a further 10 minutes until tender. Cool and arrange on a platter with the egg quarters surrounded by the watercress.

3 Beat all the sauce ingredients together until smooth. Put the sauce in a small bowl and drizzle over each individual serving of salad.

Vegetable Fritters with Tzatziki

Spicy deep-fried eggplant and zucchini slices served with a creamy yogurt and dill dip make a good, simple party starter or an excellent side dish.

SERVES 4–6
½ cucumber, coarsely grated
8 oz natural yogurt
1 tbsp extra virgin olive oil
2 tsp fresh lemon juice
2 tbsp fresh dill, chopped
1 tbsp fresh mint, chopped
1 garlic clove, crushed
salt and ground black pepper
1 large eggplant, thickly sliced
2 zucchini, thickly sliced
1 egg white, beaten
4 tbsp all-purpose flour
2 tsp ground coriander
ground cumin

1 For the dip, mix the cucumber, yogurt, oil, lemon juice, dill, mint, garlic and seasoning. Spoon into a bowl then set aside.

2 Layer the eggplant and zucchini in a colander and sprinkle them with salt. Leave for 30 minutes. Rinse well in cold water, and then pat dry.

3 Put the egg white into a bowl. Mix the flour, coriander and cumin with seasoning and put into another bowl.

4 Dip the vegetables first into the egg white then into the seasoned flour and set aside.

5 Heat about 1 in of oil in a deep frying pan until quite hot, then fry the vegetables a few at a time until they are golden in color and crisp.

6 Drain and keep warm while you fry the remainder. Serve warm on a platter with a bowl of the tzatziki dip lightly sprinkled with paprika.

Mushroom Saucers

Recipes which are already portioned are a great boon for the host, as guests can help themselves without feeling they are taking more than their fair share. Large flat mushrooms are great for this reason.

SERVES 8
8 large flat mushrooms with stalks removed, wiped clean and chopped
3 tbsp olive oil
salt and ground black pepper
1 onion, sliced
1 tsp cumin seeds
1 lb leaf spinach, well washed, stalks trimmed, and shredded
1 × 15 oz can red kidney beans, drained
7 oz soft cheese with garlic and herbs
2 medium tomatoes, halved, seeded and sliced in strips

1 Heat the oven to 375°F. Lightly grease a large, shallow ovenproof dish. Brush the mushrooms with some oil, place them in the dish and season well with salt and pepper. Cover with foil and bake for about 15–20 minutes. Uncover, drain and reserve the juices.

2 Fry the onion and chopped mushroom stalks in the remaining oil for 5 minutes until soft. Then add the cumin seeds and mushroom juices and cook for a minute longer until reduced down.

3 Stir in the spinach and fry until the leaves begin to wilt, then mix in the beans and heat well. Add the cheese, stirring until melted and season again.

4 Divide the mixture between the mushroom cups and return to the oven to heat through. Serve garnished with tomato slices.

Marbled Quails' Eggs

Hard-boiled quails' eggs re-boiled in smokey China tea assume a pretty marbled skin. It's quite a treat to dip them into a fragrant spicy salt and hand them round with drinks. Szechuan peppercorns can be bought from Oriental food stores.

SERVES 4–6
12 quails' eggs
2½ cups strong brewed lapsang
   souchong tea
1 tbsp dark soy sauce
1 tbsp dry sherry
2 star anise pods
lettuce leaves, to serve
ground Szechuan red peppercorns
sea salt, to mix

1 Place the quails' eggs in cold water and bring to a boil. Time them for 2 minutes from when the water boils.

2 Remove the eggs from the pan and run them under cold water to cool. Tap the shells all over so they are crazed, but do not peel yet.

3 In a saucepan, bring the tea to the boil and add the soy sauce, sherry and star anise. Re-boil the eggs for about 15 minutes, partially covered, so the liquid does not boil dry.

4 Cool the eggs, then peel them and arrange on a small platter lined with lettuce leaves. Mix the ground red peppercorns with equal quantities of salt and place in a small side dish.

Beet Roulade

This roulade is simple to make, yet will create a stunning impression. Ideally, prepare it in the fall when beets are at their best.

SERVES 6
8 oz fresh beets, cooked and peeled
½ tsp ground cumin
2 tbsp butter
2 tsp grated onion
4 eggs, separated
salt and ground black pepper
FILLING
⅔ cup sour cream or heavy cream
2 tsp white wine vinegar
good pinch dry mustard powder
1 tsp sugar
3 tbsp fresh parsley, chopped
2 tbsp fresh dill, chopped
3 tbsp horseradish relish

1 Line a jelly roll pan with waxed paper and then grease the paper. Preheat the oven to 375°F.

2 Roughly chop the beets, then blend to a purée in a food processor and beat in the cumin, butter, onion, egg yolks and seasoning. Turn the beet purée into a large bowl.

3 In another bowl, that is spotlessly clean, whisk the egg whites until they form soft peaks. Fold them into the beet mixture carefully.

4 Spoon the mixture into the jelly roll pan, level and bake for about 15 minutes until just firm to touch.

5 Have ready a clean dish towel laid over a wire rack. Turn the beet mixture out onto the towel, and remove the paper carefully in strips.

6 Beat the sour cream or cream until lightly stiff, then fold in the remaining ingredients. Spread this mixture onto the beet mixture. Roll up the roulade very carefully and allow it to cool.

Pasta and Beet Salad

Color is vital at a party table, and this salad is certainly eye catching. Serve the egg and avocado at the last moment to avoid discoloration.

SERVES 8
2 uncooked beets, scrubbed
8 oz pasta shells or twists
3 tbsp vinaigrette dressing
salt and ground black pepper
2 celery stalks, thinly sliced
3 scallions, sliced
⅔ cup walnuts or hazelnuts, roughly
   chopped
1 dessert apple, cored, halved and sliced
DRESSING
4 tbsp mayonnaise
3 tbsp natural yogurt or ricotta cheese
2 tbsp milk
2 tsp horseradish relish
TO SERVE
curly lettuce leaves
3 eggs, hard boiled and chopped
2 ripe avocadoes
bunch watercress

1 Boil the beets, without peeling them, in lightly salted water until they are just tender. Drain, cool, peel and chop, then set aside.

2 Cook the pasta according to the instructions on the package, then drain and toss in the vinaigrette and season well. Cool. Mix the pasta with the beet, celery, onions, nuts and apple.

3 Stir all the dressing ingredients together and mix into the pasta bowl. Chill well.

4 To serve, line a pretty salad bowl with the lettuce leaves and pile the salad in the center. When ready to serve, scatter over the chopped egg. Peel and slice the avocadoes and arrange them on top, then sprinkle over the watercress.

Gazpacho

This classic Spanish no-cook soup is ideal for taking on picnics as it can be packed straight from the refrigerator. Keep the chopped vegetables in separate pots and hand them round as an accompaniment.

SERVES 6
1 slice white bread, crust removed
cold water, to soak
1 garlic clove, crushed
2 tbsp extra virgin olive oil
2 tbsp white wine vinegar
6 large ripe tomatoes, skinned and finely
   chopped
1 small onion, finely chopped
½ tsp paprika
good pinch ground cumin
⅔ cup tomato juice
salt and ground black pepper
TO GARNISH
1 green pepper, chopped
⅓ cucumber, peeled, seeded and
   chopped
CROÛTONS
2 slices bread, cubed and deep fried

1 Soak the bread slice in enough cold water just to cover and leave for about 5 minutes, then mash with a fork.

2 Pound the garlic, oil and vinegar with a pestle and mortar or blend in a food processor. Mix this into the bread.

3 Spoon the mixture into a bowl and stir in the tomatoes, onion, spices and tomato juice. Season well and store in the refrigerator. Prepare the garnishes and store these in separate containers.

4 For a picnic, pour the chilled soup into a flask. Otherwise, pour into a chilled glass salad bowl and hand the garnishes round in smaller bowls.

Sesame Egg Roll

A Japanese-inspired idea. A thin omelet is rolled up with a creamy watercress filling and served cut in thick slices.

SERVES 3–4
3 eggs
1 tbsp soy sauce
1 tbsp sesame seeds
1 tsp sesame seed oil
salt and ground black pepper
1 tbsp sunflower oil
3 oz cream cheese with garlic
1 bunch watercress, chopped

1 Beat the eggs with the soy sauce, sesame seeds, sesame seed oil and seasoning.

2 Heat the sunflower oil in a large frying pan until quite hot, then pour in the egg mixture, tilting the pan so it covers the whole base. Cook until firm.

3 Allow the omelet to stand in the pan for a few minutes then turn out onto a chopping board and cool completely.

4 Beat the cream cheese until soft, season well then mix in the chopped watercress. Spread this over the omelet, then roll it up quite firmly. Wrap in plastic wrap and chill.

Home made Coleslaw

Forget store-bought coleslaw! Making your own at home is quite quick and easy to do – and it tastes fresh, crunchy and wonderful.

SERVES 4–6
¼ firm white cabbage
1 small onion, finely chopped
2 celery stalks, thinly sliced
2 carrots, coarsely grated
1–2 tsp caraway seeds (optional)
1 dessert apple, cored and chopped
  (optional)
½ cup walnuts, chopped (optional)
salt and ground black pepper
DRESSING
3 tbsp mayonnaise
2 tbsp light cream or natural yogurt
1 tsp lemon rind, grated
salt and ground black pepper

1 Cut and discard the core from the cabbage quarter then shred the leaves finely. Place this in a large bowl.

2 Into the cabbage toss the onion, celery and carrot, plus the caraway seeds, apple and walnuts, if using. Season well.

3 Mix the dressing ingredients together and stir into the vegetables. Cover and allow to stand for 2 hours, stirring occasionally, then chill the coleslaw lightly before serving.

Malfatti with Red Sauce

If you ever felt dumplings were a little heavy, try making these light Italian spinach and ricotta malfatti instead. Serve them with a simple tomato and red pepper sauce.

SERVES 4—6
1 lb fresh leaf spinach, well washed, stalks trimmed
1 small onion, chopped
1 garlic clove, crushed
1 tbsp olive oil
14 oz ricotta cheese
⅔ cup dried bread crumbs
½ cup all-purpose flour
1 tsp salt
2 oz Parmesan cheese, freshly grated
fresh nutmeg, grated, to taste
3 eggs, beaten
2 tbsp butter, melted
SAUCE
1 large, red pepper, chopped
1 small red onion, chopped
2 tbsp olive oil
1 × 14 oz can chopped tomatoes
⅔ cup water
good pinch dried oregano
salt and ground black pepper
2 tbsp light cream

1 Blanch the spinach in the tiniest amount of water until it is limp, then drain well, pressing it through a sieve with the back of a ladle or spoon. Chop very finely.

COOK'S TIP

Quenelles are oval-shaped dumplings. To shape the malfatti into quenelles you need two dessert spoons. Scoop up the mixture with one spoon, making sure it is mounded up, then, using the other spoon, scoop the mixture off the first spoon, twisting the top spoon into the bowl of the second.

Repeat this action two or three times until the quenelle is smooth, and then gently knock it off onto a plate ready to cook.

2 Lightly fry the onion and garlic in the oil for 5 minutes then mix with the spinach together with the ricotta cheese, bread crumbs, flour, salt, most of the Parmesan and nutmeg.

3 Allow the mixture to cool, add the eggs and melted butter, then mold into 12 small "sausage" shapes.

4 Meanwhile, make the sauce by lightly sautéeing the pepper and onion in the oil for 5 minutes. Add the tomatoes, water, oregano and seasoning. Bring to a boil, then simmer for 5 minutes.

5 When cooked, remove from the heat and blend to a purée in a food processor. Return to the pan, then stir in the cream. Check the seasoning.

6 Bring a shallow pan of salted water to a gentle boil and drop the malfatti into it a few at a time and poach them for about 5 minutes. Drain them well and keep them warm.

7 Arrange the malfatti on warm plates and drizzle over the sauce. Serve topped with the remaining Parmesan.

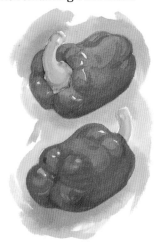

Curried Mango Chutney Dip

A quickly made, tangy and spicy dip or dressing, ideal as a dip for strips of pitta bread, grissini or sticks of fresh chopped vegetables.

SERVES 4–6
1 onion, chopped
1 garlic clove, crushed
2 tbsp sunflower oil
2 tsp mild curry powder
8 oz natural yogurt
2 tbsp mango chutney
salt and ground black pepper
2 tbsp fresh parsley, chopped

1 Gently fry the onion and garlic in the oil for 5 minutes until they are soft. Add the curry powder and cook for a further minute then allow the mixture to cool.

2 Spoon into a food processor with the yogurt, chutney and seasoning and blend until smooth.

3 Stir in the parsley and chill before serving with a variety of vegetable crudités and strips of bread.

Nutty Mushroom Paté

Spread this delicious, medium-texture paté on chunks of crusty French bread and eat with crisp leaves of lettuce and sweet cherry tomatoes.

SERVES 4–6
1 onion, chopped
1 garlic clove, crushed
1 tbsp sunflower oil
2 tbsp water
1 tbsp dry sherry
8 oz button mushrooms, chopped
salt and ground black pepper
¾ cup cashew nuts or walnuts, chopped
5 oz low fat farmer's cheese
1 tbsp soy sauce
few dashes Worcestershire sauce
fresh parsley, chopped, and a little
   paprika, to serve

1 Gently fry the onion and garlic in the oil for 3 minutes then add the water, sherry and mushrooms. Cook, stirring for about 5 minutes. Season to taste and allow to cool a little.

2 Put the mixture into a food processor with the nuts, cheese and sauces. Blend to a rough purée – do not allow it to become too smooth.

3 Check the seasoning, then spoon into a serving dish. Swirl the top and serve lightly chilled sprinkled with parsley and paprika.

Antipasti with Aioli

For a simple starter or hand-around cocktail canapé, make a bowl of the classic French/Spanish garlic sauce – aioli – and serve it with a selection of attractively prepared vegetables and breads.

SERVES 4–6
4 garlic cloves
2 egg yolks
½ tsp salt
ground black pepper
1¼ cups flavorful extra virgin olive oil
TO SERVE
red or yellow pepper, cut in thick strips
fennel, cut in slivers
radishes, halved if large
button mushrooms
broccoli florets
grissini sticks
French bread, thinly sliced

1 Crush the garlic into a bowl then beat in the egg yolks, salt and some ground black pepper.

2 Stand the bowl on a damp cloth and slowly trickle in the oil, drip by drip, whisking with a balloon whisk until you have a thick, creamy sauce. As the sauce thickens, you can add the oil in slightly larger amounts.

3 Spoon the aioli into a bowl. Arrange the dipping food around the bowl and serve lightly chilled.

Camembert Fritters

A popular snack to pass around at cocktail parties. These deep-fried cheeses are quite simple to do. They are served with a red onion marmalade which can be made in advance and stored in the refrigerator.

SERVES 4
MARMALADE
2 lb red onions, sliced
3 tbsp sunflower oil
3 tbsp olive oil
1 tbsp coriander berries, crushed
2 large bay leaves
3 tbsp granulated sugar
6 tbsp red wine vinegar
2 tsp salt
CHEESE
8 individual portions of Camembert
1 egg, beaten
1 cup plain white or whole wheat dried
   bread crumbs, to coat
oil, for deep fat frying

1 Make the marmalade first. In a large saucepan, gently fry the onions in the oil, covered, for 20 minutes or so or until they are soft.

2 Add the remaining marmalade ingredients, stir well and cook, uncovered, for a further 10–15 minutes until most of the liquid has been absorbed. Cool and then set aside.

VARIATION

You could make these fritters with fingers of firm Brie, or try it using baby rounds of goat cheese.

3 Prepare the cheese by first scratching the mold rind lightly with a fork. Dip first in egg then in bread crumbs to coat well. Dip and coat a second time if necessary. Store on a plate.

4 Pour oil into a deep fat fryer so it is one-third full; heat to 375°F.

5 Carefully lower the coated cheeses into the hot oil three or four at a time and fry until golden and crisp, about 2 minutes or less.

6 Drain well on paper towel and fry the rest, reheating the oil in between. Serve hot with some of the marmalade.

Tabbouleh 🍂

Almost the ultimate quick grain salad that simply needs soaking, draining and mixing. Bulgur is par boiled wheat. Make the salad a day ahead, if possible, so that the flavors have time to develop.

SERVES 4
¾ cup bulgur wheat
6 tbsp fresh lemon juice
5 tbsp extra virgin olive oil
6 tbsp fresh parsley, chopped
4 tbsp fresh mint, chopped
3 scallions, finely chopped
4 firm tomatoes, skinned and chopped
salt and ground black pepper

1 Cover the bulgur with cold water and soak for 20 minutes, then drain well and squeeze out even more water from it with your hands.

2 Put the bulgur into another bowl and add all the other ingredients, stirring and seasoning well.

3 Cover and chill for a few hours, or overnight, if possible.

Crudités with Humus 🍂

Always a great family favorite, home made humus is speedily produced with the help of a blender. The tahini paste is the secret of humus and it is readily available in delicatessens or larger supermarkets.

SERVES 2–3
1 × 15 oz can chick peas, drained
2 tbsp tahini paste
2 tbsp fresh lemon juice
1 garlic clove, crushed
salt and ground black pepper
olive oil and paprika pepper, to garnish
TO SERVE
Selection of salad vegetables, e.g. cucumber, chicory, baby carrots, pepper strips, radishes
Bite size chunks of bread, e.g. pitta, walnut, naan, bruschetta, or grissini sticks

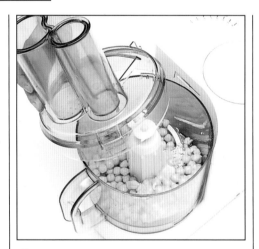

1 Put the chick peas, tahini paste, lemon juice, garlic and plenty of seasoning into a food processor or blender and mix to a smooth paste.

2 Spoon the humus into a bowl and swirl the top with the back of a spoon. Trickle over a little olive oil and sprinkle with paprika.

3 Prepare a selection of fresh salad vegetables and chunks of your favorite fresh bread or grissini sticks into finger size pieces.

4 Set out in a colorful jumble on a large plate with the bowl of humus in the center. Then dip and eat!

Index

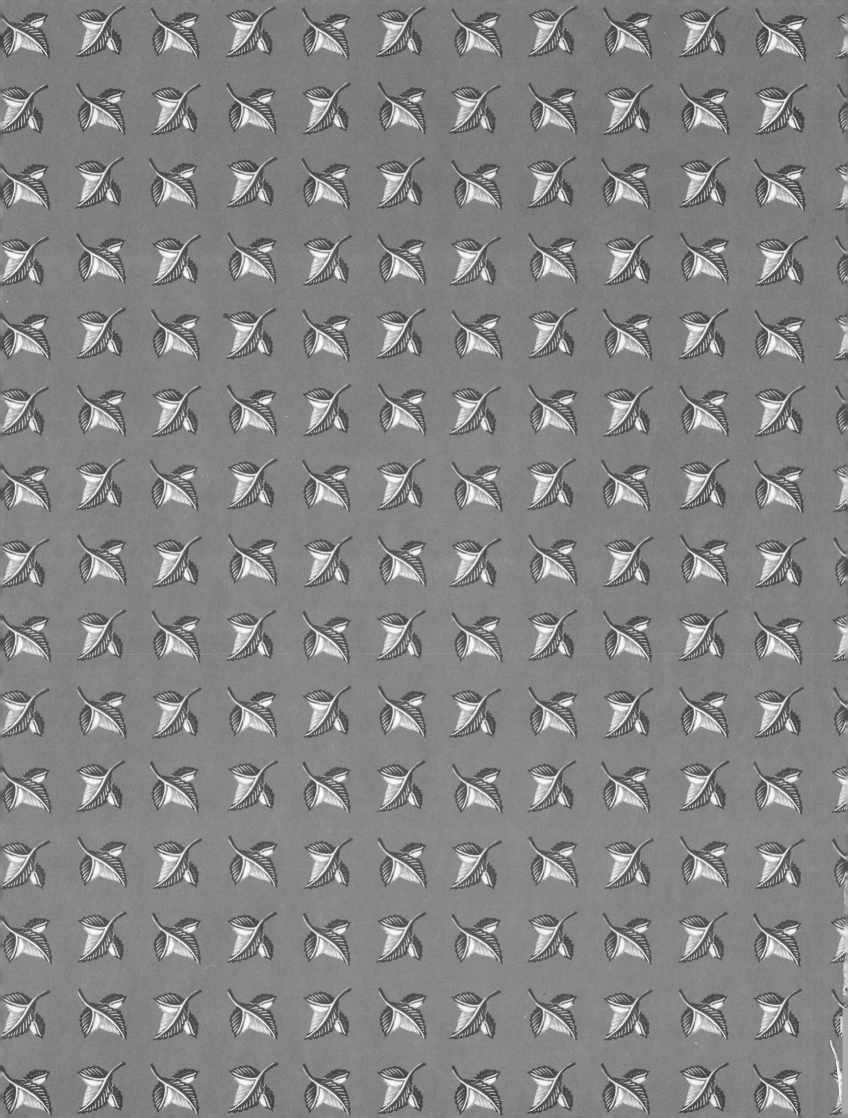